DEI

To God Most High, Lifter of My Head
Great God and Great King
The Lord of Hosts
The Lord our Maker
The Majestic God
The Sovereign Lord and Everlasting King
Hope of His People & A Very Present Help
The Lord Strong and Mighty in Battle
Eternal, Immortal, Invisible King, Only Wise God
My Helper in Whom I Trust
My Strength and High Tower
My Deliverer and Fortress
Thank you for defending Your Name
& Your Word in my life.

# ACKNOWLEDGMENTS

Special thanks to my husband, Pastor Benedict Olagunju, my best friend and my coach. Your unfailing love and inspirations have helped me to excel. To my precious and understanding children – without your support and encouragement, this book would not have been birthed.

To my spiritual son and his dear wife, Fidelis & Yemi Ukwenu. Fidelis, thank you for your constant push and encouragements. Your invaluable input day and night to this book is second to none.

To Pastor Shola Oladipupo and Joyce Edoreh, thank you for your incredible support and contributions to this book.

To my spiritual father, Apostle George Adegboye.
I am grateful for your impartations and wise counsel. To a friend (Laura) who allowed me to share her testimony of the mercy of God and power of prayer in this book. To Nonye Adeniji, thank you for spreading the revelations in Ask Volume One and Where Are Your Accusers.

To every member of Focus Centre, thank you for your prayers and your faithfulness in serving God.

# Ask

VOLUME 2

## Prayers for Everyday, Everywhere

**MINISTRY IN ART PUBLISHING**
communicating excellence

Ask - Vol. 2: Prayers for Everyday!

# Ask

VOLUME 2

PRESENTED TO

_____

OCCASION

_____

PRESENTED BY

_____

DATE

_____

For permission requests, write to the publisher, addressed "Attention: Permissions Coordinator" at the email address below:

**Ministry In Art Publishing Ltd**
e-mail: publishing@ministryinart.com
www.miapublishing.com

Unless otherwise stated, all scripture quotations are taken from the Holy Bible, New Living Translation (NLT). Other versions cited are NIV, NKJV, AMP and KJV. Quotations marked NIV are taken from the HOLY BIBLE, NEW INTERNATIONAL VERSION. Copyright © 1973, 1978, 1984 by International Bible Society. Used by permission of Hodder and Stoughton Ltd, a member of the Hodder Headline Plc Group. All rights reserved. "NIV" is a registered trademark of International Bible Society. UK trademark number 1448790.

Quotations marked KJV are from the Holy Bible, King James Version.

ISBN: 978-0-9560996-3-1

Cover design: Allan Sealy (www.miadesign.com)

# CONTENTS

# ∽ FOREWARD ∽

Many times in life we experience defeat where we should have overcome. Though initially we ask for what we want from God, we are often too weary to keep asking, to keep seeking, and to keep knocking! At times we just come short of what we desire because we stop too early in our pursuit of what we originally wanted. In this way we fail where others were able to obtain because they continued in their pursuit even when they were weary. One of the conditions for obtaining anything is not fainting in our quest for it. We need to take the risk to get the reward. Prayer can do anything God can do, for the arm of God responds to its touch. If we ask anything according to His will, we know that He hears us and because we know that He hears us, we know we have the petitions that we desire of Him.

Prayer is the key that opens the inexhaustible storehouses of divine grace and power. *"Ask, and it shall be given you!"* *(Matthew 7:7)* cries our heavenly Father, as He swings the doors of His treasure house wide open. Whatsoever we ask the Father in the name of the Son He is willing to give to us. The only limit to what prayer can do is what people do about prayer. Ask of the Lord and He shall give the heathens to you for your inheritance and the uttermost parts of the earth for your possession. To the God that hears and answers prayers all things are possible.

It is only when men bow their knees and call upon God that they become as mighty as the Almighty himself. There is a standing invitation from God that we should call unto Him and He will answer us and show us great and mighty things, which we do not know. If we pray, as we should, we would see Him work as only He can. When the outlook is bad, try the up look.

The resources of heaven are boundless, but men have limited their descent to satisfy their every craving need by not seeking Him prayerfully in spirit and truth. No matter what other things we have, if we do not pray, it profiteth nothing. The average time allotted by most Christians to prayer is deplorable and scandalous. **John Wesley**, the Father of modern day Methodism, said *'God is limited by our prayer lives because He can hardly do anything for humanity unless somebody asks Him to'*. The poverty and powerlessness of the average Christian finds its explanation in the words of the apostle James; *'Yet ye have not, because ye ask not.' (James 4:2).*

It is related of Alexander the Great that on one occasion a courtier asked him for some financial aid. The great leader told him to go to his treasurer and ask for whatever he wanted. A little later, the treasurer appeared and told Alexander the man had asked for a large sum and that he hesitated to pay out so much. *"Give him what he asks for,"* replied the great conqueror. *"He has treated me like a king in his asking, and I shall be like a king in my giving."* Oh, for the realisation of the greatness of God to whom we come in prayer!

*'Why is it,'* you may have asked repeatedly, *'that I make such poor progress in my Christian life?'* *'Neglect of prayer,'* God answers you directly. *'You have not because you ask not.'* Man of God *'Why is it that there is so little fruit in my ministry?'*

you may have pondered. *'Neglect of prayer,'* God answers again. *'You have not because you ask not.'* *'Why is it in our church, body, life and service,'* both ministers and laymen are asking, *'that there is so little power?'* And again God answers *'neglect of prayer. You have not because you ask not.'*

God has provided a life of power for every child of His by putting His own infinite power at our disposal. He has proclaimed repeatedly in a great variety of ways in His Word, *'Ask and ye shall receive.'* Those who have taken God at His word in this matter have always found it true. What are you doing with this same promise? Are you just admiring it or have you admitted it as the rule of your action?

This book calls us all to employ and deploy the weapon of prayer along with the powerful all time tools of reflections and powerful declarations to get those things that are legally ours. Take it, read it, keep it, share it and do it – this is the summation of my admonition. You will never remain the same again.

**Apostle George Adegboye**

# ≈ PREFACE ≈

God is Omnipotent, Omnipresent and Omniscient – He can do what He pleases and no being – whether celestial or terrestrial can contend with Him. However, God does nothing in the realm of the physical unless He has been invited or asked to do it otherwise He would be breaking a law – the very principle that He put in place Himself. To operate on the earth, you must have a physical body; you must be born of a woman.

For the supernatural to operate in the realm of the natural, someone (a person born of a woman, a natural person) must necessarily invite or give permission for that to happen. The devil himself can not violate this rule and therefore "possesses" people's bodies in order to carry out his work of destruction. Our God however does not override the will of any of His creatures; He is a gentle Spirit waiting for you to invite Him into your life and into your circumstance.

Prayer is our tool and means of inviting God and His supernatural power into our natural situations and circumstances. The first volume of "ASK" was laden with 40 prayer topics to help you invite God into your different circumstances. The overwhelming success and demand for the book has led to an unprecedented need for further prayer themes to cover even more circumstances and situations that affect our daily lives. Every one of us ought to have what I call an "ASK" approach to life. Only those who are confused, lost and lack a clear identity refuse to ask. It can also be said that, the person that is fearful to ask is often unwilling to gain new knowledge. No wonder the Bible says some people perish for lack of knowledge (Hosea 4:6 paraphrased).

There are 21 prayer topics in this second volume of "ASK." 21 is a multiple of the number seven, which represents perfection and liberation as well as a multiple of the number three which represents the number of the Godhead; Father, Son and Holy Spirit. In each of the prayer topics, you will find scriptures, relevant practical reflections, prayer points for your daily needs and powerful declarations that will assist your quest for a God focussed future. I trust that you will find this book useful in inviting and granting permission to the supernatural power of the Most High God to operate in your life's circumstances as did the first 40 prayer topics. I encourage you to rise up today and take hold of your future at the altar of prayer. Nobody can really do it for you, **ASK!**

# ≈ INTRODUCTION ≈

At 27 years of age, her life was already over. She was totally convinced there was nothing left to live for, all she could do now was simply to wait for death to come. Laura (not her real name) met God soon after burying her husband who had died from complications arising from HIV AIDS. She too had tested positive for HIV, having been infected by the man she loved very dearly, the man she was married to for a short five year period. This is Laura's true story...

Born to Polish parents over 27 years ago, Laura was brought up in a Christian home. She grew up to attain both a bachelor's and a master's degree in Children's Education; she qualified and trained as a teacher. She left Poland for a brief period between the years 2000 and 2001 to work in Berlin (Germany), on her return to Poland; she met a young African man who had come to work on a project in Poland. The couple fell in love and the young man stayed on in Poland after completing his project.

Laura faced serious backlash from her parents and entire family, racism remained rife in Poland at the time and as a matter of fact, her father threatened to disown her if she proceeded to marry her African boyfriend. She went with her heart and married him nonetheless. Laura even wrote a personal letter to the president of Poland at the time to plead against her husband's deportation from the country.

Her relationship and subsequent marriage to a black man made headlines all over the country; the media had a field day.

Laura's matrimonial joy was somewhat short lived. Initially she relocated to England on her own attempting to pursue a teaching career. Since her husband's immigration status was not totally settled, it seemed the best option was for him to remain in Poland. Shortly after arriving in England, she rented a room in a shared house. One day whilst home alone with one of the male flat mates, she found herself locked in against her will, and was brutally raped. Even after violating her, this man refused to let her leave the house and she eventually had to be rescued by some friends she had managed to call on her phone. The perpetrator was eventually arrested and sent to prison for his offence. During the trial of the rapist, it came to light that he had committed similar acts in the past and he was said to have had multiple sexual partners.

Following this terrible experience Laura returned

to Poland to her husband. The revelation of her rapist's reckless sexual history made Laura fearful and she immediately requested to be tested for the dreaded HIV on her return to the UK. On the day she was to receive the test results, she approached the outpatient department of the hospital but found no one there. At the far end of the room was a table with a file sitting on it, she approached the file with fear and trepidation thinking to herself, '*my God, no, let it not be....*' At that point a member of the medical team walked in and hearing her saying *no, no, no.....*the medic nodded and said 'yes, you are HIV positive.' Her world ended, it came crashing to an instant halt. She mustered up enough strength to telephone her husband who was in Poland at this time, and broke the sad news. She asked him to go and have an HIV test, her husband told her that it couldn't be, "this is AIDS we are talking about", he said.

He called her a few days later and told her he tested negative; she thanked God in utter relief and hung up the phone. A few months later, with his immigration troubles over, Laura's husband joined her in England. Things seemed fine for a few weeks and then he suddenly took ill, critically ill as a matter of fact. He was admitted to hospital and was suddenly diagnosed with paralysis, his condition worsened and he suffered both lung and kidney failure; Laura was told he had very little time to live.

He was tested again for HIV- this time the result was positive. Laura almost killed herself believing she was responsible for his illness; she had transmitted the dreaded virus to him. She was even more shocked when the doctors told her that he not only had the HIV virus, but he had full blown AIDS. They reckoned he must have had the virus for between eight and nine years! At the time of the test, his CD-4 count was 6! (The CD-4 cell count is used to measure the health of a person's immune system: a normal CD-4 count is around 600!) He was practically a dead man walking. Furthermore, she received news that the person who raped her, whom she thought infected her with the virus was tested and he came up HIV negative. In addition, her husband was found to have two other sexually transmitted diseases; these other infections were much more recent. In fact, she discovered shortly after that he had a child in Africa and another child in Poland with another woman.

At this point, Laura was distraught and tired of life, she could not believe that her husband had done this to her; that he had misled her and kept such devastating information from her all this while. Everything she thought she knew about him was a lie; her entire world came crashing down. Her husband died a few days later, for quarantine reasons, his body could not be flown home so he was cremated and she took the ashes back with her to Poland for burial. She returned to England a few weeks later believing she would have access to better medical care and that at least she could perhaps spend her last days in a fair amount of comfort. She saw no reason to live, death was knocking at her door – ready to make a rude entry, and this is when her story truly began…

Following her husband's burial, Laura returned to England with no place to stay; she went to her local council office for assistance with housing. She was given an appointment to see a housing adviser to discuss her options for housing. Now, let me go back a few steps in this story, though Laura was raised in a Christian home she had practically no knowledge of the power of God. During her short stay in England she had met a few believers who had invited her to a Pentecostal Church where she had acquired a significant knowledge of who God is and she had learnt that miracles do happen.

With the discovery that she was HIV positive and the death of her husband and a catalogue of other things going wrong in her life, she despaired and indeed began to question whether or not God existed, and if He did, why is He allowing all these bad things to happen to her. She told God that she was not a bad person, she has not done a lot of the things other people did and she had only ever slept with one man – her husband. Why was she a victim of the dreaded HIV and why would God allow her to marry a man only to end up a widow with an incurable disease? Though knocked down on the inside, she made a decision that she was going to get up. The Bible says, *'But David found strength in the Lord his God'* (1 Samuel 30:6). After days of crying and secluding herself from people, nursing and cursing all that had happened; she pulled herself together and came to the point where all she could do was to ask God for help…. help to believe in Him… help to cope with what she had to deal with. She said "God if you are real, then prove it to me in my life."

So Laura attended her appointment at her local council, little did she know that God heard her prayer, saw her pain and He was waiting to meet with her in a way she could never have imagined. She was scheduled to have her appointment in interview room 2 at the council building. The adviser conducting the interviews in room 2 on that day was a lady who did not believe in God, whilst the person scheduled to run the interviews in room 1 was a born-again Spirit filled Christian.

So on that faithful morning, Laura arrived early and waited in interview room 2 as she was the first appointment for the day. The housing adviser for interview room 2 arrived late; incidentally the gentleman for interview room 1 arrived just in time and did not bother confirming which room he was assigned to. As he walked past the reception towards the interview rooms, the receptionist told him his first appointment had arrived so he headed straight for interview room 2 assuming Laura, who was sitting patiently was his first client of the day.

He settled down and set up his laptop to conduct the interview, on accessing the interview database he discovered at that point that he was in the wrong room! He called the other adviser whose room he had taken to apologise and to arrange to swap, but she said it was not necessary and that she would just see all the appointments in room 1 whilst he could see the ones for room 2. The interview began with the adviser going through the regular routine questions, about 10 minutes into the interview, he suddenly stopped; he felt the need to ask Laura if she was a Christian. As this was not necessarily a thing he could do in the workplace, he concluded the interview, closed the laptop and told Laura he would like to ask a few personal questions not related to her housing interview if she didn't mind, Laura was fine with this. After being asked if she was a Christian, Laura simply broke down crying. She gathered herself together and told him she believed in God and how she had asked God for a sign that He is real and that He loved her.

The housing adviser spent the next 30 minutes talking to Laura about God, faith and about miracles. He explained to her how he was not meant to see her and the circumstances that led to him being the person interviewing her. Incidentally, though each interview was scheduled for 45 minutes, the second person to be interviewed for the day in interview room 2 did not turn up and this allowed both Laura and the adviser time to discuss God in some depth. She was convinced that God had set up the meeting that morning to get through to her. The adviser told her he was convinced God had a work for her to do in His kingdom and even the pain she had gone through would be useful and valuable for the kingdom. She agreed saying she believed God's plan for her life but she struggled to understand it all. Overall the housing department were unable to offer assistance of any kind that day - yet Laura left the building with a smile and a renewed desire to live for God. The adviser had given her his personal number to call anytime she felt low and needed someone to speak to.

The next few weeks turned out to be an emotional

roller coaster for Laura, on certain days she would feel great and motivated to live and to know God more, on other days, she would despair for life and would not want to speak to anyone. She rang the young man she had met at the council building regularly - sometimes several times a day; at times she would weep on the phone, at other times she just needed someone to talk to her. The young man constantly shared the Word of God with her and encouraged her to study God's Word daily. He talked to her about the power of prayer and encouraged her to pray regularly. He continually convinced her that what she was experiencing would turn out for God's glory. Laura was actually a very inquisitive young lady and asked many questions sometimes querying what she read in the Bible and in particular the love of God. Through it all she always maintained that she just desired more knowledge of God – her intent was never to call God a liar or doubt Him, she just wanted answers and God provided most of these through the man she had met and through her local church.

Laura needed a job; her desire was to be a teacher. She also needed a roof over her head. Above all, she wanted to be strong and healthy, all of which she was told was possible through Christ. She started to pray and ask God for her needs. She asked God to prove Himself in her life. First she got a job, it was not the type of job she was after but the adviser who had now become like a brother to her encouraged her not to give up. Then the housing department reversed its original position and provided her with a place to stay, additionally the hospital report confirmed her CD-4 count was holding strong. With God's help, everything she prayed for was coming to pass. After applying for teaching jobs and being rejected so many times, she was on the verge of giving up and settling for a job as a nanny. The adviser told her not to give up – he spurred her on telling her she was better than a 'nanny job'. He continued to pray for her and with her – this resulted in her being invited to an interview for a teaching assistant role.

A few days before the interview, she called her friend (the adviser) and told him she wasn't going to attend the interview, she said it would be a waste of time - like all the others, they would tell her she didn't have teaching experience in England and that her English was not good enough! Her faithful friend made her promise she would attend the interview – she did and a few hours after the interview, she was called and offered the job! That however was not the end of the matter, Laura had to undergo a pre-employment medical check, this of course involved filling in a medical questionnaire. Laura wanted to walk away from the job at that point - as she didn't want to reveal her HIV status. She asked her friend if she could leave out that information on the form but he told her to do the right thing and leave it to God. She completed the forms, sent them off and the waiting began, surprisingly to Laura, she didn't have to wait for long at all, she was contacted and given a start date without delay. She started the job and within 2 months she was made a supervisor! Soon she had taken over every major administrative and regulatory responsibility in the school! Her employers sent her for several developmental courses and she was already being positioned for a managerial role at the school.

Amidst this eventful period, Laura became very involved in her local Church. She joined the choir and ran the children's department as well. She received several prophecies that she will be completely healed of the HIV virus and she believed it! Laura boldly looked forward to having her own husband, her own home and her own children but before all of this, she became aware of a trend in her family and prophecies also served to confirm this to her. It happened that two of her aunties had been raped, her mum was also raped by an uncle, (in fact she thought she was her uncle's child) now, remember Laura had also suffered rape herself. She further considered and noted that there had been eight divorces in her family, a series of miscarriages including 3 children born alive but all died within 3 months. Her increased knowledge of spiritual things made her realise that these occurrences were not a coincidence, she believed it was a curse of some sort on her family. She sought the assistance of her pastor to overcome the trend she had noticed. Together, Laura and her Pastor fasted and engaged in a prayer regime, which was still ongoing at the time this book was published. Her Pastors' conducted a deliverance session for her and she received a Word confirming that the curse was broken!

Laura's life has been totally turned around by the power of prayer; God surely came through for her. From a place where she despaired for life and found no reason to live, to the point where she is now loving every single reason for being alive and relishing the opportunity to serve God. She has acquired a lovely car, has been the subject of advances from a couple of men and her health is just great! She has gone from strength to strength and she is totally thankful to God for her new life.

I encourage every reader of this book with this wonderful testimony of deliverance and restoration, as you read through this second book in the "ASK" series, you will surely find the motivation and encouragement to continue to pray and believe that your life is destined for glory in the name of Jesus.

# CHAPTER I

# MY WORST FEAR

It was the third death in my immediate family within a very short space of time. I could not understand what was going on. How could a brother and two sisters pass away in three separate incidents within such a short time? How could I stop this evil trend of untimely death in my family? This is my (the author's) story of deliverance...

As I share my heart with you, I am utterly grateful for God's saving grace over me. I have passed through the anguish of losing loved ones to death. I would like to submit to you that my God was and is the overarching pillar that held me; I connected with Him at the altar of prayer. Following the untimely death of my siblings, I interceded against the spirit of premature death that once afflicted my family. This is a story I believe you may be able to identify with, as well as learn from because when you think about it, you may notice some sort of a negative trend or pattern in your family.

I am the third child of the twenty something children my father had. Before my father passed away in 2002, there was no record of bereavement in the family and things of joy never ceased in our home. Now and then, we would experience some unremarkable issues not uncommon to a polygamous setting. My father was a polygamist who married five wives in his lifetime and probably had other mistresses. His relationship with his wives was characterised with pain and separation. Life was nonetheless pretty good with the mixture of joy here and there and some absence of peace.

In April 2003, I decided to go back for what I call a second chance to study Applied Social Studies.

I NOW HAD A 'RECORD' IN MY FAMILY: THREE DEATHS IN 3 CONCURRENT YEARS... THIS WAS JUST NOT RIGHT.

In the midst of my indecision whether to embark on the studies or not, I was informed that my baby sister had delivered a baby via caesarean section. It soon turned out that my sister developed a haemorrhage due to lack of proper medical care. However, when another intervention did arrive, it was very late! Two weeks post delivery, in indescribable pain, my sister eventually died on the way to hospital - she was only 28 years old. Was I not praying all the while? Oh yes, I was.

We mourned the death of my baby sister and the pain remained very fresh on my mind until couple of years later when I received total healing from my heartbroken state. Though I went about my business as usual, I was never really the same since the incident. It broke my heart because I had never experienced any death of a loved one, how much more a younger sister with whom I shared many precious moments together. I prayed fervently and interceded for my mother to be comforted as I could feel the impact on her was unbearable. Gordon Brown in his statement expressed his condolence to David Cameron who lost his son on February 25th 2009, said

*"Every child is precious and irreplaceable and the death of a child is an unbearable sorrow that no parent should ever have to endure."*

It was a sad season for me. However, I picked up the pieces and embarked on my second chance of studies.

In August 2004, I was in a Church conference when I received the shocking news that my elder (half) brother, who happened to be the first child of the family had died after months of illness. Again, we mourned and were comforted - everyone according to his or her belief. Questions as to why premature deaths prevailed in the family since the exit of our father were now being asked. Inspite of this, no one could provide a solution or put an end to this looming affliction that was plaguing my family. Friend, whether you like it or not, every family has a story. But there is a God who hears the cry of His children when they call.

While we were still recovering from the deaths of my baby sister and my elder (half) brother, I was driving home from university on the motor way (M1) one day, when I received another shocking telephone message that my immediate younger sister had just died! *Please note - that I now had a 'record' in my family: three deaths in 3 concurrent years. Moreover my immediate sister died in the same month as my precious baby sister – this was just not right.* I almost crashed the car but with God on my side, I got home safely that day, but in terrible anguish. I could feel that hell had been let loose on my family. I asked God, why? There was bitter weeping and lamentation from my mother who refused to be comforted just as it was heard in Ramah when Rachel lamented for her children because they were no more (Jeremiah 31:15).

For many days after the recent dilemma, I was in deep thought. Then the Spirit of the Lord led me to read Lamentations 5:7,

*"Our fathers sinned and are no more, and we bear their punishment."*

I decided to phone my mother and I asked her several questions for several days, unfortunately, she could only answer a few of them. Without an iota of doubt, I strongly believed that some of the evil occurrences emanated from somewhere in the spirit realm. I was unable to pinpoint where in particular but at least I had a starting point to work with according to the scripture above.

## THE FATHER'S SIN

During those incidents that happened in my family, as I meditated day and night, I realised these occurrences could be as a result of disobedience within the family and something had to be done. No one could resolve the mystery and I had no one to turn to except God. No wonder Lamentations 5:8 says,

*"Slaves have now become our masters; there is no one left to rescue to us."*

This passage tells of the fate of a dynasty where inherited sin goes unchecked. Slaves or outsiders take charge and rule over the lives of 'real' sons and daughters because some fathers have sinned. Even though it's true that the fathers may have sinned, the children have the opportunity to repent and cry to the Lord and His Word guarantees that if they do, He will hear them and turn around their captivity for good.

No wonder King Solomon remarks,

*"It is not fitting for a fool to live in luxury – how much worse for a slave to rule over princes!"* (Proverbs 19:10).

But, King Solomon, however further saw those slaves on horseback, while the princes go on foot. (Ecclesiastes 10:7). A lot of princes are in foreign countries today doing menial jobs because some fathers have sinned. It's very boring and depressing being unemployed but some have been unemployed for so long because of sins they know nothing about, sins committed by their fathers.

Many who should be owners and directors of great businesses are being tormented by evil captors who demand of them to sing the Lord's song in a foreign land. This is sad! The horse has been loosed over two thousand years ago for the benefit of God's children to ride on without stress. But some slaves are occupying stately and great positions meant for princes. The horse can represent that outstanding job/career, good wife/husband, children, talents, opportunities and so on. The Word of God says,

*"The lions may grow weak and hungry, but those who seek the Lord lack no good thing"* (Psalm 34:10).

Friend, this is worth meditating upon. When you seek God and turn to Him, He will fulfil His promise and do His part, so don't sit back and wallow in self-pity about the pain people have caused you, don't sit back and let the actions of your predecessors deny you of a better life. Do something about it from today. God has a better plan for your life, much more than you can think or imagine. However, you need to break that family curse that has been operating in your life and in your family.

# CHAPTER II

# BREAK THAT CURSE

What other people did before you were born can affect your destiny. Perhaps the hardship and challenges you are going through are not of your making, you may be totally innocent. Some of the challenges could even stem from someone else's sin of disobedience; it is possible that many of our fathers and ancestors involved themselves in occultist practices and other such demonic activities. Some of them due to their ignorance of God committed sins which have given access to the enemy to oppress their generations after them. Perhaps your lineage stems from a background where there are peculiar patterns of failure just at the brink of success; perhaps it is infertility, marital failures, or even certain illnesses, the patterns manifest in a diversity of ways. Please do not be ignorant by calling such things 'inherited' or 'family pattern' - do not settle for it with the mindset that 'it has always been like that.' Rather dig around the root of such occurrences, discern and sniff out the source.

Unfortunately for some children, their fathers died before the hand of judgment fell upon them and as a result of their father's involvement with evil practices; these children are now suffering the punishment that their parents actually deserved! The consequences of their actions have outlived them and their sins are being visited upon their innocent generations. Some parents offered sacrifices that are now speaking against generations after them. Though such persons are under a curse of the law according to the contract their parents entered into, the Bible tells us that Christ has redeemed us from the curse of the law by taking the penalties of every curse to the Cross and He nailed everything there (Galatians 3:13). If you have identified any curse operating in your life or in your family, it is time to arise in prayers and break it. It is time to say if your father or mother has suffered, you will not suffer. Why should you suffer what they suffer? This is not God's will for your life.

One day, I read in the newspaper of the sudden death of a female celebrity who died in hospital following a skiing accident. According to the journalist's account, she was quoted as saying,

*"There was so much fuss over my divorce - I was told our marriage would be cursed." I thought, 'Don't let this be true'. I've thought about it since too. I try to put*

*it out of my mind. "It was an opinion given straight to my face by someone I trusted. 'You will never be happy', he said. 'Your marriage will end in disaster'."*

Many people in our world today are operating under curses spoken against them without knowing what to do to nullify the power of that curse. Many don't even believe in the existence of curses. Many don't deserve the curse or curses working against their lives, but the Bible says that the curse causeless shall not alight and that simply means that an underserved curse will not rest (Proverbs 26:2). As

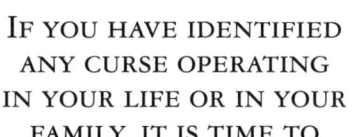

IF YOU HAVE IDENTIFIED ANY CURSE OPERATING IN YOUR LIFE OR IN YOUR FAMILY, IT IS TIME TO ARISE IN PRAYERS AND BREAK IT.

soon as you are aware of any curse being placed on you or perhaps recognise one or two effects of any such curses, then, it is time to do something about it. Any attempt to ignore it or take it with a pinch of salt can result into calamity. This female celebrity was noted as saying she did not believe in the curse but took it simply as media speculation. Just like this lady, have you disregarded curses spoken against you? Instead of renouncing an evil pronouncement spoken against you, have you simply overlooked it?

God's Word expressly highlights that the benefits of

obedience lead to blessings whilst the consequences of disobedience lead to curses (please take time to read Deuteronomy 28). Life therefore, is a matter of choice but God in His infinite mercy did counsel us to choose life (Deuteronomy 30:19). In the final analysis, the decision is yours as to how you choose to live your life. No matter how you have been living your life, God has promised to answer you when you call on Him in times of trouble and He will deliver you. More importantly, the reason why Jesus came was to destroy the effect of every curse (1 John 3:8).

The onus is upon you to renew your faith regarding what He came to do on the Cross of Calvary so that you will no longer walk under those curses but walk in the covenant blessings of God. The Bible says in Colossians 2:14,

*'You were dead because of your sins and because your sinful nature was not yet cut away. Then God made you alive with Christ. He forgave all our sins. He cancelled the record that contained the charges against us. He took it and destroyed it by nailing it to Christ's Cross'* (NLT).

This means, every precept of law that you have been unable to reach or keep has been removed and destroyed at the cross. Therefore, get ready to break every curse in your life and that of your family. Get ready to loose every bond of affliction emanating from the effect of the curse. Then, where you have been operating under any curse, you will begin to walk in the covenant blessings of God and there shall be open heavens. No curse shall work against you anymore in Jesus Name.

### ∼ UNUSUAL MATTER REQUIRES UNUSUAL MEASURE ∼

Throughout this unfortunate crisis in my family, I never lost my faith in God, I never stopped worshipping Him. I stayed focussed on God's promises and remained unshaken in my faith in God. I delved into the Bible for encouragement, insight and directions. I considered the story of Job and realised that what I was dealing with was an unusual matter that would require an unusual measure. The Bible says,

*"For we are not fighting against people made of flesh and blood, but against the evil rulers and authorities of the unseen world, against those mighty powers of darkness who rule this world, and against wicked spirits in the heavenly realms"* (Ephesians 6:12).

As a result of this, I sought for the permission of my husband to go away for three days into a solitary place of prayer, to appeal to the Highest Ruler and Authority of both the unseen and seen world for only He has Power over all to intervene and put a stop to this evil occurrence. The three days of fervent prayers and fasting elapsed, I faced my Father and earnestly waited to hear from Him. To the glory of God, total victory came and the Lord said unto me; refrain your eyes from weeping my daughter, this affliction shall not arise again. The regime of withdrawing to a solitary place to seek the face of God has now become my way of dealing with issues of life. I truly believe according to God's Word, that,

*"If my people who are called by name, will humble themselves and pray and seek my face and turn from their wicked ways, then I will hear from heaven and will forgive their sin and will heal their land (2 Chronicles 7:14)."*

God is faithful! My land has since been healed to the glory of His Name. Friend, do you need healing and restoration in your land? Then humble yourself and pray. Let your faith be greater than your physical sight. Remember, only the just shall live by faith. The power in His Word transcends beyond what the mortal mind can comprehend. He is the Word that dispels every power of the wicked. This same Word was used in creating you and your world. You do not need to pay anyone to use it. You can use it through asking from today. Therefore, ASK!

## ∼ THE CURSE WAS BROKEN ∼

From that year forward, the Lord has been faithful to His promise. Not only did God groom me in the discipline of prayer with fasting, I also embarked on thorough worship in order to access the throne room of mercy. I experienced deliverance for the whole family by renouncing and destroying every sin and ancestral curse that stemmed from paternal and maternal sources.

THE POWER IN HIS WORD TRANSCENDS BEYOND WHAT THE MORTAL MIND CAN COMPREHEND.

Many destinies have been aborted because people don't know that there is a price to pay to break evil covenants and curses. Someone said, 'a life without sacrifice is an abomination.' Nothing is free in life. In fact, Jesus had to pay with His Blood to redeem us from the curse of the law. To live a successful life, you must be ready to offer sacrifice of worship and sacrifice necessary time to pray. It is rather unfortunate that some Christians actually assume that since we belong to God, there is no need to pray or pay any sacrifice as it has been paid in full. One of the prices for living a successful life is prayer. Prayer needs to be a routine part of our lives that must be adhered to continuously. Josh Billings remarked:

*"Consider the postage stamp; its usefulness is limited to its ability to stick to something until it gets there."*

Therefore, act like a '1st class postage stamp believer' and be confident that you and your prayers will get to their assigned destination. Remember, you are a solution to someone's problem. What you do today will be history tomorrow so be relevant and be a history maker. Develop an intimate relationship with your Maker and be diligent in your affairs. Then,

*"He will command His angels concerning you to guard you in all your ways…When you call upon Him, He will answer you, He will be with you in trouble and will deliver you and honour you. With long life, He will satisfy you and show you His salvation"* (Psalm 91: 11, 15-16).

# CHAPTER III

# HE KNOWS
# WHAT YOU NEED

A couple planning and preparing for their wedding party needed a cow to complete the plans for their wonderful day, however, the help they needed was not forth coming. They had run out of money and the day of the wedding was fast approaching. Then the bride-to-be looked up to heaven and said 'God but it has been said that the cattle on a thousand hills belongs to you,' (Psalm 50:10) why don't you just send one to us out of the thousands. The next day someone gave her a call asking her to come for a cow. Of a truth as Billy Graham puts it,

*"Heaven is full of answers to prayers for which no one ever bothered to ask".*

What you can see, is what you will possess, so see something and you will get it, see nothing and guess what? Yes you guessed right – you get a big fat juicy nothing! Also take note that if you view situations around you from the wrong perspective, you will always be fearful. Your attitude towards an issue will determine how successfully you will to handle it.

Many people quit when they should instead persist in their demands. You are destined to ask and receive, you must be unrelenting and sober minded - Don't throw in the towel too soon – *the fight aint over yet!* The human nature readily prefers to have prayers answered on the spot - instantly. However, we should be mindful that God is not an ATM machine where you insert your card, followed by your pin number and just receive cash even though you have no money in the account. You can only make withdrawals where you have sufficient cash deposits or an overdraft facility on the account.

With God don't be surprised that you have to wait in some cases before you get a result and He always has a reason for directing you to the waiting room. Please know that your attitude whilst waiting is crucial too, be sure to adopt the mindset of worship during this period. Alternatively, God sometimes answers prayers instantaneously too or even before you open your mouth to ask, its His prerogative – that's why He is God. Dear reader, this passage of scripture is noteworthy for meditation –

*"For I know the plans I have for you says the Lord.*

*"They are plans for good and not for disaster, to give you a future and a hope"* (Jeremiah 29:11 NLT).

## ∽  PRAYER IS A GATEWAY  ∼

Prayer is an excellent, yet free gift we have been given, it is our access in the Name of Jesus, to the Most High God. Though everyone can pray without having to pay a fee, yet the simple art of praying can earn you a great deal of reward because the Bible says that effectual fervent prayer

ONE THING IS CERTAIN IN LIFE – IF YOU HAVE NEVER ATTEMPTED SOMETHING IT CANNOT WORK FOR YOU – THIS APPLIES TO PRAYER.

makes tremendous power available. Prayer is a request for God's supernatural intervention in your situation and the answer to prayer is God's display of His power in the earth. When you learn the art of praying, you will discover that it develops an enormous intimacy that attracts the presence of God into your life. The Bible says,

*"Be still, and know that I am God; I will be exalted among the nations, I will be exalted in the earth!"* (Psalm 46:10).

God is to be exalted over and above everything in life. When you believe there is no need to pray but rather indulge in complaining and murmuring, you are actually exalting that situation. A life without prayer is like living in darkness without light. Are you weary and carrying heavy burdens? Prayer will lighten your burden. Are you stagnant and confused? Prayer will elevate you and give you access to the throne of grace. Are you seeking for guidance and direction? Prayer will lead you into the centre of God's will. Are you operating under closed heavens and all your labour seems to go in vain? Prayer will open the doors and windows of heaven for you and you will see God pouring out His blessings so great that you won't have enough room to contain it.

One thing is certain in life – if you have never attempted something it cannot work for you – this applies to prayer. If you have never attempted to pray before, how would you be able to tell whether there is someone above who hears and grant requests made to Him through prayer? The Bible says,

*"Delight yourself also in the LORD, And He shall give you the desires of your heart"* (Psalm 37:4).

To delight is to enjoy or have pleasure in what you do. Knowing and serving God should not be a burden but a pleasure. After giving your life to God, constantly aspire to know more about Him. There is a lot of enjoyment to savour in His presence and that is where He gives you the righteous desires of your heart. Beware, because many love to conform to the world's standard, they love to seek God when it is convenient for them, when they have time, when they get that holiday, when they get that contract, when... when... when...

A LIFE WITHOUT PRAYER IS LIKE LIVING IN DARKNESS WITHOUT LIGHT.

## ✑ PRAYER REQUIRES FOCUS ✑

Prayer can be likened to a pregnant woman and there are several outcomes to pregnancy. A pregnant woman can have a miscarriage or stillbirth, another can give birth to a baby naturally and another by use of various types of assistive aids e.g. forceps or caesarean section. A large proportion of pregnancies are terminated before full gestation - these we know as miscarriages or abortions.

Like a pregnancy, prayers can have different outcomes, however, prayers in this book are like babies delivered naturally with only one help – and that is God.

Think about a pregnant woman in labour. As a matter of fact, she is not bothered by who is looking at her as

LIKE A PREGNANCY,
PRAYERS CAN HAVE
DIFFERENT
OUTCOMES

she pushes, pants, screams and heaves – you see there is only one reason why she's going through that pain, and that is to give birth to a baby! All that this woman needs to do is to concentrate, focus and push until the baby comes out. Friend, if you embark on prayers without looking up to God for an answer to prayers for example, you may lose that baby (request). If you embark on prayers but out of laziness give up requesting when you should be interceding, then your answer may be aborted or lead to a stillbirth. To get an answer to your request, you must focus on God and keep on believing Him until you receive an answer.

Pregnancy as referred to here may symbolise your heart desire. It could symbolise God's wonderful promises to you and to achieve them, you will need to look up to God without wavering. Perhaps you need to change your environment for a better concentration. Look for a positive and peaceful atmosphere to talk to God and hear Him clearly. As you labour in prayers, let your focus be on God, knowing that with Him you will rise above life's challenges in Jesus Name.

# CHAPTER IV

# THE HINDRANCE OF UNFORGIVENESS

Unforgiveness is like excess baggage/weight, its ugly and not worth carrying about. It is a waste of your precious energy. Unforgiveness will hinder your prayers; it will close the heavens over you and make your worship unacceptable (Matt 5:23; Mk 11:5). Forgive every person who victimises, slanders or accuses you because when you walk in forgiveness, you create an atmosphere of distinction for yourself, an atmosphere where the supernatural can operate. Taking revenge for yourself will create a circle of pain, the devil is ever so happy to be a constant reminder (or should I say accuser) of your refusal to forgive each time you kneel down to pray.

Each time you stand to pray, the accuser protests with placards informing God about your excuses of what others have done to you and to point out how you are living in unforgiveness. To be frank he would have a valid reason as to why God should not listen to your supplications. You have to forgive and stop carrying around a heavy burden of resentment. Henry Ward Beecher remarked,

*"Forgiveness has to be like a cancelled note; torn in two, and burned up, so that it never can be shown against one."*

Unforgiveness will hold you down, it is one power the devil uses against you. The Bible reminds us in John 14:30,

*"...for the prince of this world came to search out whether there was any fault in our Lord Jesus Christ" However, he found nothing and had no hold on the King of hosts" (paraphrased).*

Friends, there is absolutely nothing the prince of this world (the devil) can do if after searching you out, he finds nothing (unforgiveness) in you. He cannot hinder you and even if he afflicts you, know for sure that your Redeemer lives.

## ❧ FORGIVE NO MATTER THE OFFENCE ❧

Forgiveness is crucial if you are to provoke the presence of the Almighty and walk in total freedom. The heavy weight of unforgiveness disfigures you, drags and pulls you down when you do nothing but live in constant bitterness. Unforgiveness when

IT IS IMPOSSIBLE TO HUG SOMEONE WITH YOUR ARMS FOLDED AND THE SAME GOES FOR WHEN YOU EXPECT TO RECEIVE ANSWERS TO YOUR PRAYERS.

left to fester leads to resentment, this then progresses to bitterness - a bitter man is a dangerous man. It is impossible to hug someone with your arms folded and the same goes for when you expect to receive answers to your prayers. Here are some practical ways of forgiving those who have betrayed you, hurt you and caused you grief and heartache. It worked for me and I believe it will work for you too:

- Resolve in your mind to forgive no matter the offence
- Take out a blank piece of paper
- Write the name(s) of the person(s) who have hurt you, grieved you or accused you wrongly, the list goes on
- Try to remember or ask the Holy Spirit to remind you of each offence from that person
- Now begin to confess with your mouth as you write the following words: I forgive and release from my mind (mention the name of the person)
- It's like a breathing exercise, as you let it flow out of your mind, you are actually exhaling

anger, bitterness, resentment, pain, unforgiveness and all of that negative baggage you harbour on the inside. When you inhale after exhaling, you breathe in freedom, peace, happiness, joy, total forgiveness and this is the reason why you have to let go and let God.

• Finally, hand over the matter to God. For sure, He will judge accordingly.

## ⋙ HE WILL AVENGE YOU ⋘

HATE, BITTERNESS AND REVENGE ARE LUXURIES NONE OF US CAN AFFORD. FORGIVE YOUR ENEMIES AS YOU CANNOT GET BACK AT THEM ANY OTHER WAY!

**~John Mason**

One of the secrets to a peace-filled existence is to forgive. If you can eliminate unforgiveness from your life, you will have peace with God which surpasses every understanding. On the other hand, many are constantly crafting plans of vengeance and are bent on their pursuit of taking revenge which only leads to more pain. Revenge is only sweet when you leave it to God. You may not know it, but your enemies will always carry the burden of the pain they caused you, it is something their minds will rehearse and nurse throughout their lifetime, this is perhaps part of God's "vengeance."

The story of Joseph and his brothers in the land of Egypt was a typical example of a 'sweet revenge.' I wish we could see the countenance of those brothers worn out by famine and hunger when Joseph revealed his identity and announced to them that,

*"I am Joseph!"..."Is my father still alive? But his brothers were speechless!"* (Genesis 45:3).

What a rematch! I bet they were all trembling with their heads bowed. They thought they had sold him off to slavery and that he would never reappear. Throughout the ordeal, Joseph went from one storm to another with no record of bitterness. Meanwhile, the revealer of all truth and the deliverer Himself was working behind the scenes on behalf of Joseph. When the time of vindication and payback came, the rewarder of every wicked deed took vengeance for Joseph and it was delectably sweet and better coordinated than anything Joseph imagined.

The brothers could not believe their eyes as they saw God in action. As the thoughts and pains of their evil plot against Joseph were still being rehearsed in their minds, Joseph showed them love; he asked them to draw near. He used the opportunity to remind them of how they sold him as a slave into Egypt – how could they forget! God's vengeance was so intense that even Joseph could not avoid feeling sorry for them. He encouraged them not to get angry or get bitter with each other as everything had worked out in his favour. The Bible reaffirms,

*"Dear friends, never avenge yourselves. Leave that to God. For it is written, "I will take vengeance; I will repay those who deserve it," says the Lord"* (Romans 12:19).

Therefore, I encourage you to let go and let God handle the payback, it may not be according to your own timing but leave it to God. Ecclesiastes 3:1 says,

*"There is a time for everything, a season for every activity under heaven."*

When the time and the season for God's vengeance to descend upon the enemy comes, you will be amazed! However, do not gloat with pride but give glory to your heavenly Father for fighting your battle, lest the table turn against you. I totally agree with John Mason when he said,

*"Hate, bitterness and revenge are luxuries none of us can afford. Forgive your enemies as you cannot get back at them any other way"!*

That is a profound statement. Forgiveness is the only way to get revenge.

# CHAPTER V

# THE PRE-EMINENCE OF HIS WORD

During the regime of fasting and fervent prayers that I embarked upon to break what I thought was probably a curse over my family, the Lord constantly impressed upon me the need to emphasise the concept of the integrity of the Word – God's Word.

As I meditated day and night on God's Word, the following scripture became so real to me: John 1:1-5,

*"In the beginning the Word already existed. He was with God, and He was God. He was in the beginning with God. He created everything there is. Nothing exists that He didn't make. Life itself was in Him, and this life gives light to everyone. The light shines through the darkness, and the darkness can never extinguish it"* (NLT).

Since life itself was in the Word and this life gives

light to everyone, I encourage you to speak the Word more frequently.

Please join me to acknowledge and declare the pre-eminence and greatness of the WORD:

- The Word created everything and never dies.
- The Word never fades or fails.
- The Word is supreme and eternal.
- The Word does not knock before it enters  through the door of the mighty.
- The Word is sharper than a sword and it pierces through the heart.
- The Word penetrates through hidden and secret places.
- The Word can lift up and can cast down.
- The Word is the source of every success.
- The Word is the beginning and the end.
- The Word is life and death.
- The Word will always succeed concerning everything for which it is released.
- The Word turns situations around and reverses every evil thing for good.

Proverbs 18:21 says,
*"Death and life are in the power of the tongue, and you will eat the fruit thereof."*

Since words can kill or nourish life, let the right words always proceed from your mouth. Some words have kept people in captivity and have been used negatively to hide people in obscurity

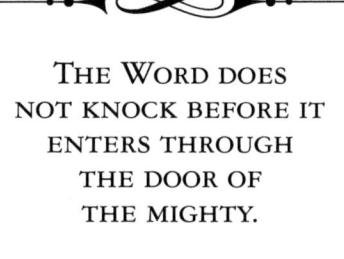

THE WORD DOES NOT KNOCK BEFORE IT ENTERS THROUGH THE DOOR OF THE MIGHTY.

and bury their goodness and potential. Irrespective of any evil pronouncement of wicked words against you, God is bringing you into prominence in Jesus' Name.

## BELIEVE GOD'S REPORT

As long as you are available and faithful, you can leave the rest to God. He knows best and He will do it for you. The days of doubting and believing the lie of the devil that God cannot save you are over. Listen to this: Steve Wulf wrote in the Time Magazine (November 25, 1996) what Mike Tyson (a Moslem) said after he lost the fight to Evander Holyfield in an 11th-round TKO:

*"I got caught in something strange," said Tyson. Or something wonderful, depending on your viewpoint."*

No wonder the Bible says,

*"For the Lord shall rise up as in Mount Perazim, He shall be wroth as in the valley of Gibeon, that He may do His work, His strange work; and bring to pass His act, His strange act"* (Isaiah 28:21).

Holyfield had been described as an "underdog" prior to his fight; did you know that the Nevada State Athletic Commission was so worried about his heart irregularity that it would not sanction the fight unless he received clearance from the Mayo Clinic? Yet he went into the fight with great determination. Holyfield believed the report of God and proved professionals wrong. He made history in his lifetime.

Here is his testimony from the Time Magazine to ginger and encourage you. God is no respecter of persons. If He has done it before, He will do it again. He holds the whole world in His hands and He is able:

*"Nobody thought I could win," Holyfield said last Friday during a swing through New York City. "Their judgments were not based on our talents, though, but on our images. It was the monster with hate in his heart versus a man who was always talking about God. But the Bible tells us to have no fear, and I didn't. Besides, I've known Mike since I was 17. He's not so bad."*

This is amazing! Remember, I said earlier that there is a need to know your God and then you will become a threat to the kingdom of darkness.

Choose those with whom you associate carefully – i.e. your friends, confidants, lifetime partner and even business partners. One of the reasons why Evander Holyfield won that fight is not far from Steve Wulf's report in the Time Magazine that says:

*"Also in his figurative corner was his new wife, Dr. Janice Itson, an internist from Chicago whom he met several years ago at a revival meeting. Midway between the Olympics and the fight, Holyfield asked her to marry him – and to help take care of his finances as well as his six children by four different women. Not only did she restore order to his Atlanta household, but she also gave her husband a new sense of well-being. "I never could've beaten Tyson without Janice.'*

Truly, passion is contagious and magnetic - you can only attract a character synonymous with your own. Note: Holyfield met his wife in a revival meeting – yes I said revival meeting! Gals and guys, who are still single and searching, be mindful of where you go in your pursuit for an eternal partner. Prayerfully ask God for guidance and direction and He will direct your steps.

##  CONFESSION BRINGS POSSESSION

The Bible says,

*"Now the Lord God had formed out of the ground all the beasts of the field and all the birds of the air. He brought them to the man to see what he would name them; and whatever the man called each living creature, that was its name"* (Genesis 2:19).

As Adam was given the authority and opportunity to rename all the beasts of the ground and the birds of the air, so have you been given the same authority and opportunity to rename every challenge representing a beast in your life. When the enemy says there is a casting down, you rename it and declare that there is a lifting up. When the enemy declares lack into your life, you rename it and confess abundance. When the enemy calls you single, rename that singleness, confess that you not alone. Our heavenly Father is an extraordinary God, if He said, it is not appropriate for the man to be alone, then He will divinely connect you with a suitable partner as He did for Eve (Genesis 2:18). Therefore, begin to liberate yourself as you rename

WHEN THE ENEMY SAYS THERE IS A CASTING DOWN, YOU RENAME IT AND DECLARE THAT THERE IS A LIFTING UP.

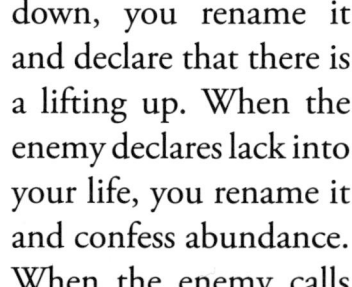

all those challenges. Be stirred up and begin to visualise precisely what you want to possess because only the just shall live by faith.

## ∾ POWERFUL & PIERCING WORDS ∾

When faced with undeniable trials and challenges that seem very difficult to handle, adopt the strategy of David which he used when he was confronted with Goliath's challenge. The Bible says,

*"As soon as the Israelite army saw him (Goliath), they began to run away in fright. Have you seen the giant?" the men were asking. "He comes out each day to challenge Israel…"*

May I just pause here to say that in our world today, we face different giants like Goliath manifesting as challenges of barrenness, failures, miscarriages, health issues, financial crisis and the list goes on. Many are living in fear just like the Israelites, seeking help where there is none. Many have even thrown in the towel and given up serving the only true God.

Have you been going through the same challenge day after day, week after week, month after month and year after year? Child of God don't just stand there - confront the challenge in prayer, this is truly the easiest way to victory. Though, David may have been small in physical stature and Goliath indeed very big in stature, in the spirit realm, little is much with God. Right in the middle of the battle, David confronted Goliath with some very powerful Words that were sharper than the sharpest knife. The words of David pierced through the heart of Goliath as he said,

*"You come to me with sword, spear and javelin, but I come to you in the name of the LORD Almighty – the GOD of the armies of Israel, whom you have defied (I Samuel 17:45).*

These were words uttered with sole reliance on God; they pierced through the heart of Goliath and weakened him even before David hurled the stone from his sling that hit his forehead. Oh! What a sight it must have been - just to see the countenance of Goliath when David spoke those powerful and piercing words. Goliath felt belittled by David but still underrated what young David could do. He viewed David as a mere midget in His sight. What this giant failed to see was the power behind the spoken words of David.

## ∽ GOD HAS A PLAN FOR YOUR LIFE ∼

If you had foresight into the devils plans, you would realise that you cannot afford to be lukewarm or weary. You can not allow discouragement to come in because if you do, the fire goes out completely and you will have no strength to fight. The devil knows when to top-up the storms and trials in people's lives. He does it at a time when they are most vulnerable. Vulnerability can occur when we are in our comfort zone or when we experience discouraging times. However, God has a better plan for you than what you are going through.

What you are currently facing is not the end of the matter. If the issues of twelve years in the life of that woman with the flow of blood could end in one day (Mark 5:25-34), surely issues in your life shall come to an end in Jesus' Name. The plan of total freedom for that woman was eventually fulfilled. For the first time in twelve years, she experienced perfect health and peace. She recovered her dignity and liberty to live a quality lifestyle.

Your life is not an accident, what you have is a planned life. God has divinely designed your life and there is an appointed time and season for your manifestation. I know waiting can be frustrating for us mortal beings - especially when we want to know the 'when', 'how' and what He will do. The Word of God says,

*"But those who wait on the Lord shall renew their strength; they shall mount up with wings like eagles…'* (Isaiah 40:31).

Therefore sit back, relax and wait. While waiting, occupy your place in destiny and do other profitable things. Prayerfully ask God for strength to do the impossible. To fight the battles of life, you need strength and the Bible counsels,

*"If you fail under pressure, your strength is not very great"* (Proverbs 24:10).

But I pray for you that you will not faint in the day of adversity. When you need to stand up and fight, you will not lack the strength to arise no matter how intense the pressure, in Jesus' Name. Now, get up, it is time to pray and begin to live a life of purpose and significance.

# Chapter VI

# THE PRE-EMINENCE OF PRAISE

A key secret to successful prayer is the readiness and ability to give praise to the Most High God. Thanksgiving is simply the art or act of giving thanks; it is the fitting way to approach the Father and the proper way to enter into His presence. The Bible says,

*"Enter His gates with thanksgiving; go into his courts with praise. Give thanks to Him and praise His name" (Psalm 100:4 NLT).*

Anyone who intends to receive answers to their prayers must cultivate the habit of being thankful for everything, especially for little things; things I like to refer to as 'little mercies'. Even when things seem to be difficult and you are in the midst of trials or pain, thank God that you have not lost everything. When you allow the voice of your praise to be stronger and more frequent than your voice of petition, then you will have set the platform for all the requests you intend to make.

At times, we are guilty of taking the goodness of God in our lives for granted. We take it for granted that we are going to see tomorrow, we take it for granted that when our children go out to school, they will return home. We take it for granted that when we set out on a journey, we will arrive safely. We even take for granted the air we breathe in as well as being alive. We take the fact that we have friends for granted, the fact that we can walk for granted and the fact that we have water to drink for granted. When you approach God, and you want answers to your prayers, you put yourself in a good position when you start by thanking Him for the things you do have before you ask for the things you do not have.

Whenever you pray, make it a point to start by thanking God for the little mercies (don't forget the big ones too!), give Him praise for His goodness in your life. Even if you are about to pray a prayer of warfare, praise has to go forth from your lips first, listen to what God told the Israelites

*"And the children of Israel arose, and went up to the house of God, and asked counsel of God, and said, Which of us shall go up first to the battle against the children of Benjamin? And the LORD said, Judah shall go up first"* (Judges 20:18).

Judah in the Hebrew language means Praise. Can you see the pre-eminence of praise in that scripture? On the way to the battle, God said Judah a.k.a. praise must go forth first!

## WHEN EVERYTHING ELSE FAILS

In Genesis 29 (NLT), we read about Leah the daughter of Laban who became the first wife of Jacob. Leah felt unloved by Jacob as she was never his first choice. Jacob preferred Rachel instead. Leah, who suffered from a deep-rooted attention seeking syndrome, spent most of her life producing children, hoping to get Jacob's affection and attention. Similarly, there are many in our world today who suffer the same disposition. Some will go to any extent to buy other people's affection to get attention. So Leah devised a strategy to have her way. She became pregnant, had a son and named him Reuben, saying, her husband will now love her. Not too long after this, she conceived again, had her second son and named him Simeon, for she said, the Lord heard that she was unloved. Soon after that, she became mother to another son and named him Levi, for she said with confidence that her husband will now give her his long awaited-affection. Yet, Jacob did not fulfil Leah's expectations in all of her devices! Eventually, she made up her mind about what to do with her next pregnancy. She became pregnant, had another son but named him Judah, for she said,

*"Now I will praise the LORD! And then she stopped having children"* (Genesis 29:35 NLT).

Like Leah, you may not be loved or appreciated and people may not give you their attention. Well, it is time to make a U-turn and give birth to praise. The Bible says,

*"Rejoice evermore. Pray without ceasing. In every thing give thanks for this is the Will of God in Christ Jesus concerning you"* (1 Thessalonians 5:16-18 KJV).

Friend, don't waste your precious time and energy trying to be men-pleaser. When everything else fails or frustrates you, allow praise to take the lead. William Ward counsels that,

*"There are three enemies of personal peace: regret over yesterday's mistakes, anxiety over tomorrow's problems and ingratitude for today's blessing."*

In spite of disappointments and crisis, choose to maintain your identity and to be joyful. God's mercies are new every day – so what if people may not care or love you as you want them to?

For a very long time, King David was extremely depressed and refused to neither eat nor drink because of his sick child that was born to Bathsheba in the act of adultery. Eventually, the child died! Surprisingly, the king got up, had a

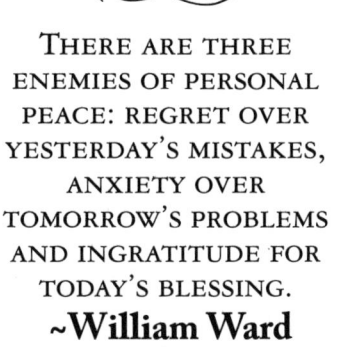

THERE ARE THREE ENEMIES OF PERSONAL PEACE: REGRET OVER YESTERDAY'S MISTAKES, ANXIETY OVER TOMORROW'S PROBLEMS AND INGRATITUDE FOR TODAY'S BLESSING.
**~William Ward**

good shower (in scented bath oil) and changed his garment of heaviness for a garment of praise. The Bible says,

*"...and came into the House of the Lord, and worshipped"* (2 Samuel 12:20 KJV).

In typical King David style, get up off the floor and stop weeping, instead worship the Lord who knows better. He has a better plan for you. In all the predicaments of Job, the Bible says he did not sin but worshipped the Lord. The purpose of the wicked is to scatter your praise (Zechariah 1:21) so that you will not lift up your head. Irrespective of any setbacks you have suffered, never lose your praise. Where every thing else has failed, praise God continually and watch the devil go hang himself while your joy comes! Now get ready to ASK.

# 21 PRAYER TOPICS

Ask - Vol. 2: Prayers for Everyday!

## YOUR CHILDREN'S FUTURE

*And I will establish My covenant between Me and you and your descendants after you throughout their generations for an everlasting, solemn pledge, to be a God to you and to your posterity after you.*

Genesis 17:7 (AMP)

*Their descendants shall be known among the Gentiles, And their offspring among the people. All who see them shall acknowledge them, That they are the posterity whom the LORD has blessed.*

Isaiah 61:9 (NKJV)

*Therefore may it please You to bless the house (posterity) of Your servant, that it may continue before You forever; for what You bless, O Lord, is blessed forever.*

1 Chronicles 17:27 (AMP)

## REFLECTION

I watched a telecast by Jesse Duplantis, a renowned man of God. On this particular broadcast he spoke of his book entitled "Close Encounters of the God Kind", he spoke about how God "bothered" him as he grew up. He said that he was the so called "black sheep" of his family and that his mother often introduced him as her "little heathen", because according to him, he never understood God and never believed.

He grew up to become a successful rock singer and was constantly on the road to-ing and fro-ing between gigs and shows. Even though he never believed in God, he explained that from a tender age, he had 'experiences' of God. At the age of nine, he once told his teacher that God followed him everywhere but the teacher did not understand what he was talking about. Poor child, they probably classed him as needing psychiatric attention. But he definitely knew and he could sense God's presence around him. Isn't that awesome? When Jesse turned 17 years old, he was involved in a ghastly car accident. Prior to the accident his mother had told him how she had a vision about him and she saw a tide of the Blood of Jesus sweeping over him. Being the radical that he was he told his mum to stop all this God talk and that he did not believe in that stuff. But mummy dearest just told him like it is "Tough luck Jesse that you were born to me" she said, you are going to serve God whether you like it or not!

When God wants your attention, He can and will pull all manner of stunts to reach you. The man of God wrote that his car was damaged beyond recognition in the accident and made newspaper headlines, but as the car somersaulted, he felt a hand on his shoulder, holding him back on his seat. That single act of God stopped a metal piece which broke from the steering wheel from piercing through his body. After this encounter Jesse Duplantis still went on to become a rock artiste. He stated that sometimes as he got ready for his shows, he would feel God's presence; instinctively he would call his mother to say, "momma are you praying? Quit praying!" and bang the phone in annoyance. Another time he records, he was at a bar getting high with his friends when he suddenly heard God's voice saying "get out of the bar." He told his friends that God said they should get out of the bar and he left. He called his mother who told him "God told me you are in a bar somewhere and I told Him to tell you to leave, did you hear His voice?" He said yes and I left! Have you noticed that in all these episodes, the young man in spite of his rebellious streak would always obey 'that voice', even though he did not understand or believe. That is the covering of the power of a prayerful parent.

Eventually, the rebel that has become one of the greatest men of God in our generation today, Jesse Duplantis became born again in his bathroom whilst on tour playing rock concerts. I sincerely believe it is the intervention of God by virtue of the persistent prayer of his mother. He went on stage that night and instead of singing the usual lyrics to his rock music he changed the wording and sang "everybody in this place is going to hell." He quit his rock band that night and is now a renowned evangelist for the most High God!

God promised not only to be our God, but that His covenant blessing will remain valid forever (Genesis 17:7). More than that, He said He would bless us to the extent that our whole dynasty will continue forever before Him (1 Chronicles 17:25-27 NLT).

Like the mother of Jesse Duplantis, we have to take full responsibility to pray for our children and their future. When we take charge of their future in prayers, no matter how hard the devil tries, God's Hand will be strong upon them and keep them for the covenant's sake! For it has pleased the Lord to watch and direct them in such a way that every where they go and in everything they do, our children will always recognise God's presence with them and eventually succumb to His Lordship over their lives.

Do you have a child or children playing truancy in some form or fashion? I implore you to allow the testimony of this man of God to encourage you to pray without ceasing for your children. It does not matter whether your children are little or grown up or even if you are still in the process of planning to have them. It is never too early or too late to start setting the stage for the future of your children. The Bible says, "The earnest prayer of a righteous person has great power and wonderful results" (James 5:16 NLT). Prayer is telling God your righteous desires for your children; as long as these are Word-based be sure that it's a 'done deal'.

## PRAYER POINTS

- I decree and declare that my children shall pursue excellence in all their outward appearance – their speech, conduct and demeanour shall be to the glory of God's Name.

- Lord let Your Hand rest mightily upon every one of my children. Let them serve You in their lifetime, let my womb and my offspring be an asset to You Oh Lord God in the Name of Jesus.

- Let my descendants, all called by name be known and be recognised throughout all ages because of

Your Hand and Your blessing upon them. Let all who see them acknowledge that they are blessed by You in Jesus Name.

- Let Your blessings never depart from my house Oh Lord. Let Your blessing permanently remain upon my lineage because that which You have blessed is blessed forever.

- God of all ages, let my children be delivered from the destruction of this age, let their enemies not go unpunished Oh Lord but let their deliverance be of You, total and complete in Jesus Name!

- My Father and my God I use the testimony of Jesse Duplantis as a point of contact; that You will never depart from any one of my children or descendants, even those who seem rebellious.

- Lord, according to Your promise, draw every one of my children to You. And by the power of the Blood, deliver them from a sinful generation unto Yourself in the Name of Jesus.

## MY PROPHETIC DECLARATION

In the Name of Jesus, I decree and declare that all of my children will know the Lord and serve Him. They will recognise Him only as God all the days of their lives. I decree that the presence of the Most High God will never depart from any of my offspring no matter where they are or what they are up to.

Your Word confirms that the gifts and the callings of God are without repentance. I thank You therefore for choosing my family to serve You. I thank You Lord that Your calling upon the life of every member of my family and my lineage will be fulfilled in the Name of Jesus. I declare and decree that the entire stock of my household will know You and serve You all the days of their lives in Jesus Name.

Lord, I decree that You will arrange for good the circumstances of my children, their children and their children's children, throughout all generations. I decree in advance that they shall marry the bone of their bone and flesh of their flesh. You will direct their footsteps so that they may serve only You all the days of their lives in Jesus Name.

I boldly state the following: that as the Lord lives, none of my children will be lost to the kingdom of darkness in the Name of Jesus. None of my children will walk in the ways of sinners. None of my children will sit in the seat of the scornful and none of my children will walk in the counsel of the ungodly by the precious Name of Your Son Jesus.

# TRIUMPH OVER INJUSTICE

*Those who plant injustice will harvest disaster, and their reign of terror will come to an end.*

Psalm 22:6 (NLT)

*Trust in the LORD with all your heart, And lean not on your own understanding; In all your ways acknowledge Him, And He shall direct your paths.*

Proverbs 3:5-5 (NKJV)

*Then the Lord asked Satan, "Have you noticed my servant Job? He is the finest man in all the earth – a man of complete integrity, even though you persuaded me to harm him without cause."*

Job 2:3 (NLT)

## REFLECTION

Whilst we see tragedy and suffering in the story of Job, we must bear in mind that we live in a fallen world where good conduct is not always rewarded, neither is bad conduct always punished. When we witness a notorious criminal prospering or an innocent child suffering, we conclude and say, 'that's not right.' Of a truth, sin has twisted justice and made our world unpredictable and unattractive.

Have you ever been wrongly accused or wrongly denied of something that should ordinarily have been yours? Perhaps you've been incarcerated for a crime you did not commit, or even worked hard towards a dream only to have it crumble at the last minute? Maybe you've been in a relationship for years which you expected to lead to marriage; then suddenly before your very eyes, it fell apart? Have you committed your money into the hands of a trusted one to supervise a project for you - only to be swindled with no one to confront the unscrupulous trickster? Situations like this occur everyday with no explanation, nevertheless, no matter what pains or setbacks you have suffered, God is just and merciful. He is a God of recompense; He will intervene and give you double for the trouble you have suffered. The Bible tells of many who endured such injustices – but do you know what? They overcame when they cried and asked for God's divine intervention.

The plan of the enemy is to orchestrate assorted problems in your life in order to enslave you, but you will not serve the enemy in Jesus' Name. Such perverse miscarriages of justice have caused many people to serve lengthy prison sentences, only to be later released for lack of evidence or some other legal technicality that is serving the purpose of the enemy! I read in the newspaper recently of a man who had been imprisoned for 27 years only to have his sentence reversed because there was an error in the original judgement! The media used the right words to describe it – miscarriage of justice! There are lots of people who have been sentenced unjustly like that man and deprived of their liberty. Some have appealed against the injustice suffered and had their cases quashed, whilst others have not been so fortunate.

Nonetheless, there is a God who rules in the affairs of men. He is the God of all man-kind and nothing is too difficult for Him. Any act of wickedness or injustice committed against you regardless of its source or size, is an enemy destined to be confronted and conquered by all means. We live in perilous times where injustice and wickedness are prevalent. If you are in a situation where someone has taken it upon themselves to be unfair and cruel to you; just hold your peace! The Bible reassures us that, '... *when you grow restless, you will throw his yoke from off your neck*' (Gen. 27:40). Is there any injustice or act of wickedness making you restless right now? The best way to exit your dilemma is to stand up tall and demolish their yokes in prayer! Then you will triumph over every wicked act of injustice against you in Jesus name.

## PRAYER POINTS

- Pray and decree that you will not be a victim of miscarriage of justice in any form neither a victim of someone else's error.

- Make a bold pronouncement that you will not serve the enemy, and will never be deprived of your valuable time.

- Pray that your dreams and desires will not be aborted. Decree that your expectations will not be cut short but instead each one of them will be fulfilled by the grace of God.

- Demand that every act of injustice and every form of oppression be broken from your life.

- Pray against every wicked calculation designed to inflict harm upon you unjustly.

- Ask the Lord for the wisdom and direction to bring everything before Him, and particularly for wisdom to seek His help for every situation.

- Earnestly ask the Lord to order your steps both

in motion and direction. Pray and ask Him to deliver you from every trap of the enemy.

## MY PROPHETIC DECLARATION

God of recompense! I decree and declare that I am strong and I am not afraid. I believe you will come with vengeance to save me. When the enemy comes in like a flood, I declare that Your Spirit shall lift up a standard against him. I am not a candidate for oppression in the name of Jesus; I am a candidate for mercy, justice and truth in the Jesus name! I terminate every reign of terror, injustice and every act of wickedness over my life and my family.

By faith, I shall overcome every attempt of false accusation, miscarriage of justice and imprisonment. I declare that I will not serve the enemy on things I know nothing about! I will not be denied nor deprived of my liberty. When ruthless witnesses come forward; my Father in heaven shall rescue my life from their ravages. O Lord, awake and rise to my defence! Help me to see the mighty flood of Your proof of favour in my affairs and in the life of every member of my family.

I declare that You are my hiding-place; You will protect me from every trap of the enemy. I will acknowledge You in all my ways and delight myself in You. I declare that my expectations shall not be cut off forever in the Name of Jesus. My aspirations and my purpose in life shall not be aborted in Jesus name.

# 3

## TURNING HOPELESS SITUATIONS AROUND

*Against all hope, Abraham in hope believed and so became the father of many nations, just as it had been said to him, "So shall your offspring be."* Rom 4:18 (NIV)

*Now faith is the substance of things hoped for, the evidence of things not seen.*

Hebrews 11:1 (NKJV)

*For whatever is born of God overcomes the world. And this is the victory that has overcome the world—our faith.*

1 John 5:4 (NKJV)

## REFLECTION

Hope is important for human existence, especially in the lives of those who put their trust in God.

We have learnt that we receive from God by faith, and that if we ask anything from God and do not doubt in our hearts, we will receive those very things that we ask of Him. It is unfortunate, but the element of hope is often overlooked by many. Beloved, please understand that where there is no hope, faith has nothing to work with! The Bible clearly states that faith is the substance of things we hoped for. The New Living Translation puts it this way, "Faith is the confidence that what we hope for will actually happen; it gives us assurance about things we cannot see" (Heb 11:1 NLT). So, when all looks hopeless, look to God exclusively.

The Bible tells of an excellent man called Job, this faithful man suffered terrible pains through no obvious fault of his own - indeed we still see such instances in the world even today. However, Job's story did not end in hopelessness. From the beginning to the end of his life we can see that faith in God is justified even when our situations look hopeless. To be unshakable, faith must be built on the confidence that God's ultimate purpose will come to pass. A person, whose focus is directed toward the world, will find it hard to know when God intervenes. It is not the plan of God for you to live in constant despair, His plan for you is of peace and not of hopelessness.

Let's consider Abraham – a prime biblical example of a person who was in a hopeless situation but did not give up. The Bible says he was childless at 99 years old and not only that, "it had ceased to be with Sarah after the manner of women". This simply means that Sarah's menstrual cycle had stopped! Her ovaries were defunct of egg production so even if Abraham still had any seed in him at 99, Sarah had no eggs to receive the seed! Clearly, their quest for a child was hopeless! Abraham however, held on to the Word of God against hopelessness. He maintained his hope and the Bible records that he became strong in faith because he counted God who had promised him a child to be faithful. Of course we know the rest - at 100 years old, Abraham had a son. His wife, Sarah at 90 years old miraculously began to ovulate; she sustained a pregnancy and brought forth Isaac! God is the God of hope! So don't let anything cause you to give up hope!

Friend, He who lives in you is greater than any hopeless situation. No matter the circumstances, choose to hold on to God's Word which says, Christ in you, the hope of glory (Colossians 1:27). Psalm 145:18 further admonishes us that "The Lord is near to all who call on Him…" Therefore, be hopeful and stand in faith remembering that if God could do it for Abraham and many others, He can and will resolve that hopeless situation of yours. Above all, be fully persuaded that, *'God has the power to do what He has promised'* (Romans 4:21).

## PRAYER POINTS

- Pray and break every spell of hopelessness in your life. Decree that whatever makes your life to lack direction be far from you.

- Pray and pull down every stronghold of hopelessness that leads to anxiety and worry.

- Pray and decree that you will not sink any deeper into despair. Ask God to uphold and empower you with strength during this trying time and fill you with hope that endures.

- Pray and decree that you will not be at the mercy of the wicked forces operating in the world today.

- Banish every spirit of fear and terror from your life and your heart. Command the confidence that the Word of God brings into your situation.

- Pray and ask God for a restoration of all your expectations in that situation.

- Declare by faith that you will overcome that hopeless situation and everything else that weighs you down.

## MY PROPHETIC DECLARATION

Possessor of heaven and earth, you are my hope, my shelter and my strength. I declare in the Name that is above all names that I will not allow my heart and mind to be troubled, discouraged or disturbed. My faith is unshakeable. My hope is built on nothing else, but on the power of Your Word oh Lord! I will hope in Your powerful Name for it is more precious than gold. I declare that in the face of what seems to be hopeless, I am full of hope and I hope in Your mercy. The flood shall not overwhelm me neither will the deep waters swallow me. You will rescue me oh Lord from those who hate me. Pull me out of despair and anguish. In Your unfailing love, O God, pull me out of this mess. By Your saving power, help me to live in joy and show me favour.

Because you live, I declare I can face tomorrow and I therefore rest my hope on Your unfailing love to bring to pass all You have promised. Let there be a manifestation of my expectations. By virtue of your greatness and by faith, I declare my victory over that hopeless situation. I refuse to be controlled by dejection and discouragement. Because I am born of the Almighty God, I am lifted out of the pit of hopelessness. For the Lord has planted me like strong and graceful oaks for His own glory!

# 4

## HANDLING CONFLICT AT WORK

*Yet He did not let anyone oppress them. He warned kings on their behalf: "Do not touch these people I have chosen, and do not hurt my prophets."*
1 Chronicles 16:21-22 (NLT)

*Because of the oppression of the weak and the groaning of the needy, I will now arise," says the LORD. "I will protect them from those who malign them.*
Psalm 12:5 (NIV)

*When you go through deep waters, I will be with you. When you go through rivers of difficulty, you will not drown. When you walk through the fire of oppression, you will not be burned up; the flames will not consume you.*
Isaiah 43:2 (NLT)

### REFLECTION

God is your creator. Did you know that makes you His prized possession? The Bible says, *"…even the very hairs of your head are all numbered"* (Matt.

10:30). Numerous theologians suggest that this verse basically means that each hair on your head is uniquely numbered such that, if one strand of hair falls from your head, He knows exactly that it was hair number 2,154 that fell! That is how much God cares about you and how precious you are to Him! He is so passionate about you that He gave an explicit instruction that no one should oppress or harass you!

Have you ever noticed that some of the most miserable people in the world are lazy people? They are not diligent about their home, work or business affairs. They are sloppy and careless putting in minimal effort but expecting maximal praise! They are constantly at loggerheads with their managers, always blaming everyone but themselves for their misfortune in the workplace! The Bible says, 'do you see a man who is diligent in his work? He shall stand before kings and not stand before mean men' (Prov. 22:29 paraphrased). Mean men are people of notorious reputation. They are wicked taskmasters who are ruthless and have no regard for anyone. However, if you are diligent in your work or business and you have paid the price of hard work, be rest assured that the Lord is by your side to confront and conquer any challenge or conspiracy that you may face.

Vince Lombardi wisely counsels that, "Success is like anything worthwhile – it has a price. You have to pay the price to win and you have to pay the price to get to the point where success is possible. Most importantly, you must pay the price to stay there – do not try to cheat the system; it only leads to more trouble and shame. Once you agree upon the price you and your family must pay for success, it enables you to ignore the minor hurts, the opponent's pressure, and the 'temporary setbacks' – of which there may be many. No matter the magnitude of pressure or challenges in your workplace or business, it's a price that must be paid as a winner. What you need to do as God's precious child is to be still and watch Him handle the matter for you – be still and be faithful, leave the rest to Him. After all, He has already warned kings and bosses on your behalf and He has promised to be with you in whatever situation you are going through. With your knees bowed and your mouth fervently pronouncing His Word, relax and hold your peace.

This testimony will encourage you: A lady in her place of work was constantly harassed and victimised by her so called manager. After several disciplinary meetings and warnings without cause given to her, as she was on the verge of unfair dismissal, finally, she took the matter to the highest Authority with prayers and fasting. This unrelenting lady stood on the Word of God according to Lamentations 3:35-37, "To turn aside the justice due a man before the face of the Most High, or subvert a man in his cause – the Lord does not approve. Who is he who speaks and it comes to pass, when the Lord has not commanded it?" Standing on those words, she prayed and fasted for some days. Somehow, something happened between the manager and another member of staff and guess who quit? The manager! Today, the same lady is flourishing in her job with excellent prospects ahead of her. Beloved, anytime you feel oppressed or hindered in any area of your life, be it toward your career, business, projects, marriage or studies, just take your stand and pray!

It is crucial for any managers reading this to be fair and be careful how you treat God's precious children who are working for you because they have a God who jealously guards them. For He will not allow anyone to oppress or hurt them! Managers do not abuse your authority – treat your team as you would like to be treated, you too will surely reap the rewards of this in more ways than one.

## PRAYER POINTS

- Pray and destroy any power raising problems against you at your workplace. Ask God to deliver you from any form of antagonism.

- Pray and decree that every person, whether a colleague or a manager oppressing you and making life difficult for you will be visited by the Lord. Decree that no conspiracy shall succeed over your job.

- Pray that the very person that hates and victimises you and seeks your downfall shall henceforth be at peace with you and promote you.

- Pray and declare that you will not be intimidated but you will be bold and be strong in spite of every act of bullying or harassment in your place of work.

- Pray and decree that as the mountains surround Jerusalem, so shall the Lord surround you with overwhelming peace and favour.

- Pray and demand that your job will remain secure irrespective of the actions of any boss or colleague in the office.

- Pray that every one that digs a pit for you in your workplace will turn round and fall into it themselves. Prophesy that everyone plotting your elimination shall subsequently be eliminated.

## MY PROPHETIC DECLARATION

O Lord, I have come to you for help. You are my sun and shield. You are my light and my salvation. You are the strength of my life and I shall not be afraid of anyone. You will give me grace and glory in my place of assignment. I declare I am not moved by what I see or hear. I am safe and secure in my job. Because my trust is in the Lord God of Hosts, I am like mount Zion, which cannot be removed! As the mountains are round about Jerusalem, so is my heavenly Father round about me. I will be fruitful, faithful and resourceful in my job – I will not be idle. I will not be a cheat or unfaithful to my managers. I will epitomise diligence in all tasks committed to me in Jesus' Name.

I decree and declare that no weapon formed or fashioned against me shall prosper! Every effort to conspire against me or set me up will not succeed! My heavenly Father, who is strong and mighty in battle, will frustrate and shatter every wicked plan to eliminate me. Everyone who places an obstacle before me will trip over it themselves and anyone who digs a pit to cause me hurt will fall into it in Jesus Name. I declare that when it is time to leave my present place of work, it will be because the Lord has elevated me to something much better and peaceful. Every yoke of oppression around me is broken by the power of the Most High God.

He that keeps me will neither slumber nor sleep. The Lord is my keeper, the shade upon my right hand. I shall escape every snare of the fowler and the enemies within that lay in wait for my downfall. I declare that my job and my affairs are safe and protected from devourers. My job is protected by the Name of the Almighty! His Word and His Blood have secured my job and I am at peace in Jesus Name!

# 5

## COPING WITH CHANGE

*Therefore we will not fear, though the earth should change and though the mountains be shaken into the midst of the seas.*

Psalm 46:2 (AMP)

*But those who wait for the Lord [who expect, look for, and hope in Him] shall change and renew their strength and power; they shall lift their wings and mount up [close to God] as eagles [mount up to the sun]; they shall run and not be weary, they shall walk and not faint or become tired.*

Isaiah 40:31 (AMP)

*He changes times and seasons; he sets up kings and deposes them. He gives wisdom to the wise and knowledge to the discerning.*

Daniel 2:21 (NIV)

## REFLECTION

Change as they say, is the only thing that does not change. Many of us assume that nothing in our lives should ever change. This is probably because we are afraid of what tomorrow holds. Change is inevitable and occurs throughout all aspects of human existence. However and above all, God is the only being that never changes.

As long as we live in this world, we will experience change and we will have to deal with it. Some changes we experience are predictable and we envisage them on the horizon. For example becoming a parent is a foreseeable change. Pregnancy, which lasts for approximately 9 months (all things being equal) allows sufficient time to plan and prepare for the change that is about to take place. Some other changes are more acute and occur without prior warning e.g. losing a job/being made redundant or certain health related changes and even death.

Whether the change we are experiencing is predictable or abrupt, God's unchanging Word covers it. He reminds us in Daniel 2:21 that, *'He changes times and seasons…and He gives knowledge to the wise and discerning.'* God's Word offers us the secret to successfully deal with life's changes, this secret is apparent when you place your life firmly in His capable hands. Those who therefore wait on the Lord, even in the midst of a sudden change shall renew their strength - they shall be revitalised on every side.

Most people who are experiencing change in the natural become discouraged and dejected. But if they would only wait on the Lord and hope in Him, they will receive the strength that is needed to cope with the change. Sometimes this is easier said than done, trust me, I have been there! But God does not lie. He will equip you with necessary tools to deal with your changing situation in this changing world. Indeed, through the change that you are experiencing you will be lifted up and raised up to higher dimension of blessing!

In spite of human nature and mortal needs those who trust in God are not expected to deal with change as 'ordinary people.' Our confidence is of the Lord says the Psalmist, therefore, God's people must not fear. *'Even though the earth should change and the mountains are tossed into the sea'* (Psalm 46:2). Every promise God has made, He will carry through and as He swore by Himself, His Word will not return to Him void without accomplishing its purpose. The devil might be roaring and the storms of change might be raging fiercely; these are all scare tactics of the enemy - remember God's Word remains sure. You must therefore wait on God in the midst of your change. Job said, *'until my change comes, I will wait on Him'* (Job 14:14).

Inevitably when change does finally manifest,

move with it and you can be assured that it will work out to your advantage because *all things work together for good to them that love God, who are called according to His purpose* (Romans 8:28). So in the midst of that tempest of change, hold on to God's Word, wait on Him for strength to deal with the situation and above all, listen close to His heart for discernment and wisdom.

## PRAYER POINTS

- Pray and ask the Ancient of Days, to arm you with strength to deal with the present change taking place in your life.

- Ask and plead for God's mercy for easy transition in the area you are expecting a change in your life (name the situation).

- Pray and ask for the Spirit of discernment and the necessary wisdom to deal with that change (name the situation) in your life in Jesus Name.

- Pray and ask God to set you free from every fear of the unknown associated with this change.

- Ask God to help you adapt to the change quickly and decree that this change will bring increase, benefit and peace into your life.

- Decree that just as the storm is a platform for the eagle to soar higher and higher; that this change will be your platform to reach glorious altitudes in Jesus Name.

- Pray for strength to focus on what lies ahead and decree that you will not struggle with adjusting to the change.

## MY PROPHETIC DECLARATION

God of eternity, You are the only unchanging God, the unchangeable changer in every situation. Change this present situation around for my benefit according to Your will and purpose for me in Jesus Name.

I declare and I decree that as I go through this change (call it by name), I will wait on the Lord as He renews my strength in the Name of Jesus. I declare that this change will serve to take me higher. Like the eagle, I will mount up on wings and soar high above the storm of this change into my destiny. I will ride on the storm of this change unto greater heights in the mighty Name of Jesus.

As the Lord reveals wisdom and grants me discernment to deal with this change, I will rest on His unfailing Word of peace. This change will not lead to sorrow but shall be for my benefit and my increase. Since I am born of You Lord and because You live in me, my heart will know no fear as a result of any change. I declare that no matter how fierce the tempest of the storm, no matter how bad the change may seem, it will work out for my good because God loves me and I am called according to His purpose in the mighty Name of Jesus.

As I wait expectantly for this change to come into my life, I decree that my strength will be renewed like an eagle. By faith, I decree that change will come with total peace in Jesus Name.

# OVERCOMING IMPOSSIBILITIES

*But Jesus looked at them and said to them, "With men this is impossible, but with God all things are possible.*

Matt 19:26 (NKJV)

*Elisha replied, "Hear this message from the Lord...! By this time tomorrow in the markets of Samaria, five quarts of fine flour will cost only half an ounce of silver... The officer assisting the king said to the man of God, "That couldn't happen even if the Lord opened the windows of heaven...!"*

2 Kings 7:1-2 (NLT)

*Jesus said to him, "If you can believe, all things are possible to him who believes.*

Mark 9:23 (NKJV)

## REFLECTION

There was a season of famine in the city of Samaria, the famine was particularly severe because king Ben-Hadad of Aram had besieged the city and the king of Samaria did nothing about it (2 Kings 6:24-33). The cost of living shot up steeply and depression loomed in the land. The city had entered into a deep recession. The famine worsened to the extent the people began killing and eating one another's children since there was nothing else to eat and no money to spend. Unemployment struck the whole city and in desperation many sold their property and moved back to the village. Some even dipped into their investments to buy food and forgot about their plans for a better tomorrow. Desperation had set in and things had taken a major downturn. Eventually the king of Samaria decided to do something; however, he focused on the wrong person. He foolishly vowed to destroy the solution to his country's dilemma, prophet Elisha.

It is pertinent to be aware of the kind of decision you take in a situation like this. Many have turned against the assigned helpers of their destiny by erroneously assuming that these helpers are the cause of their dilemma. Such people have truly missed out on God's best because of their irrational reasoning. This, of course, is a setup of Satan. When things are becoming so impossible to resolve, be careful how you react - *fight the issue and not the person.*

After Elisha gave the message of hope in 2 Kings 7:1-2, officers working with the king said it was impossible for the words of Elijah to come to pass, they doubted the prophet's word They said it was impossible for the economic situation to improve in view of the sharp decline that prevailed. The message of hope from the Lord to the people (including the faithless officers) declared: "By this time tomorrow in the markets of Samaria, five quarts of fine flour will cost only half an ounce of silver..." When God speaks, something happens in the realm of the Spirit. The impossible becomes possible. The natural becomes supernatural and the ordinary becomes extraordinary.

I encourage you not to lose hope and faith regarding this current economic situation. Rid your mind of negative thoughts of impossibility and actively seek new opportunities that will advance your cause. See with fresh eyes that the economic situation of your country will improve. See your marriage blossoming and growing in peace. See yourself getting that job and prospering on every side. See yourself living a healthy lifestyle. See your womb bustling with children! Go ahead, open your eyes and see your business thriving even while others are complaining, say it is possible! Don't confess or agree with negative people that things are tight or things are difficult. With man, some things may be impossible but with God Almighty nothing is impossible.

Therefore, no matter what the economic situation of the world may be saying today; if God has declared that you will not beg for bread then He will make provision for you. Whenever you are faced with an impossible situation, go into the realm of *'by this time tomorrow'* and hold on to that declaration for your deliverance. It does not matter whether you are unemployed; go into the realm of *'by this time tomorrow'* and hold on to that declaration for your new career. You may be struggling with your health, your bills, maybe the children are running you rugged…to be honest it does not matter what your situation is… hold on to God's declaration that: *'by this time tomorrow'* your story will change for the best and you will sing a new song and dance while those who thought God cannot rescue you will watch with their faces covered in shame!

## PRAYER POINTS

- Pray and declare that every ancient gate of impossibility and limitation be lifted that the God of possibilities may step into your situation.

- Pray and ask the Lord Jesus to destroy any power that has besieged the flow of your finances! Ask God to confirm His Word in your life.

- Pray and break every curse of impossibility in your life and family. Decree that though the situations before you may seem impossible, you will not doubt what God has spoken concerning you.

- Seeing that the King of Samaria accused the man of God, Elisha wrongly, pray and decree that the devil will not succeed in setting you up against your solution to the impossible situation before you.

- Name every situation of impossibility in your life and pray in faith that every one of those situations will be turned around.

- Open your mouth and prophesy that: '*by this time tomorrow*' (make your pronouncement in faith and mention every area you are asking for God's deliverance).

- Boldly prophesy that by the mercies of the Almighty, you will walk in the corridors of power and achieve great things.

## MY PROPHETIC DECLARATION

I believe the Word of the Most High God. What He has spoken to me, He will fulfil. I go into the realm of His Word and I decree and declare that:

By this time tomorrow, I will recover all that I have lost! I receive the anointing of a winner! This is my season of possibilities. The time to favour me has come. I terminate every siege of impossibilities in my finances, health, career, marriage (mention any additional names). Whatever stops the mercy of God from overflowing into people's lives shall be far from me. Every demonic force of doubt and unbelief shall not prosper over my life. I take authority over every ancient door of limitation. I command them to lift up their heads for the supernatural intervention of my heavenly Father to happen in my life. By this time tomorrow; I will walk into the promises of God for my life. It is written, nothing is impossible with God. Therefore, my conception has been made possible. My bringing forth is possible and my business is thriving in the name of Jesus! Divine success shall attend to all that I do.

I declare that the promises of God for me will be fulfilled in my lifetime. I shall not be in the company of doubters who will hear about good things but not see it. I shall possess my possessions and the seal of the Lord of hosts shall perform it! Every righteous desire in line with the will of God that I have been praying for, I now declare them granted and established! There is no enchantment or divination that will work against me. With God on my side, I declare that all things are possible in Jesus Name!

## LEADERS & THOSE IN AUTHORITY

*I urge, then, first of all, that requests, prayers, intercession and thanksgiving be made for everyone, for kings and all those in authority, that we may live peaceful and quiet lives in all godliness and holiness. This is good, and pleases God our Saviour.*

I Timothy 2:1-3 (NIV)

*Everyone must submit himself to the governing authorities, for there is no authority except that which God has established. The authorities that exist have been established by God.*

Romans 13:1 (NIV)

*The king's heart is like a stream of water directed by the Lord; He turns it wherever He pleases.*

Proverbs 21:1 (NLT)

## REFLECTION

It is true to say that we either have deeply rooted political inclinations and alliances, or we really are not in the least bit bothered who is in power.

Some are staunch supporters of their leaders and monarchs, and some may be indifferent whilst others firmly dislike those in charge of their countries' affairs. Irrespective of what your inclinations are and whether or not you like your leader, Romans 13:1 clearly states that "the authorities that exist have been established by God" and everyone must submit themselves to the governing authorities.

Understand that the authorities being spoken about are not limited to the leaders of your nation; it includes leaders of all kinds in every area of life. So, this includes your manager in the office, your local councillor or representative, your parents and not to forget your pastor.

God's Word says that we must of a necessity lift up our voices in prayer for these people who are in a position of authority. All manner of prayers must be offered on their behalf, the Bible clearly list the types of prayers that must be said for these ones... requests, prayers, intercession and thanksgiving! We must ask God to grant wisdom to our leaders and make requests to God for their assistance. So whether or not you know or like your leader is immaterial, you must thank God for him or her regardless!

Note that there is a benefit for praying for our

leaders, the Bible says that if we pray and intercede and render thanks for our leaders, then we will live peaceful and quiet lives; and then we will live in all holiness and Godliness! Does this mean that if I do not pray or give thanks for my leaders I am being unholy and ungodly? Does it mean that I could lack peace and quiet if I do not intercede for my leaders? Well, according to the word of God, Yes! John Ruskin once said, "When a man is wrapped up in himself, he makes a pretty small package." Therefore, always thank God for your leaders and pray for everyone in authority. Learn from an Indian proverb which says, "Good people, like clouds, receive only to give away." One of the ways to be a blessing is to live a life of intercession. Did you know that you are often blessed with more time on your hands than some of our leaders? It is often said – *uneasy lies the head that wears the crown*– think about it. Martin Luther said, "I have so much to do today that I shall spend the first three hours in prayer." Nonetheless, be like the cloud and offer prayers on their behalf as you never know who is praying for you also. I fully support the adage that says *time spent in prayers is never lost* - make the most of every opportunity. Today might be the only currency you have in your pocket. Therefore, sow it or spend it well by praying and invoking the presence of the highest Ruler to be manifested in the inner chambers of your leaders when they sit or lay down to take decisions that will affect you and your family. Having done your part be assured that, "The king's heart is like a stream of water directed by the LORD; He guides it wherever he pleases" (Proverbs 21:1).

## PRAYER POINTS

- Pray that every one in every nation, who are called by the Name of the Lord, will humble themselves and pray, and seek God's face and turn from their wicked ways. Plead for God's mercy and ask Him to harken to petitions made and heal your land.

- Pray for your leader, ask God to give him or her wisdom to lead your nation through the present situation that your country is experiencing.

- Pray for all the decision makers in your country, the legislative arm of government, the ministerial cabinet of government and even the judicial system; that God will be present in their deliberations and be the Voice of Christians in every meeting.

- Give God thanks for your manager in the office and all those to whom you have to report. Thank God for placing you under their authority at such a time as this and thank God that they are placed there for your benefit.

- Intercede on behalf of the leaders in your life, for the leaders of your nation, your local councillor, your manager, your pastor and even your parents. Ask God to give them the ability to deal with every issue in their life and to grant them the grace to handle the responsibility placed on their shoulders.

- Make a request on behalf of your leaders, if you are aware of any particular issues that they have to grapple with at the present time, make a direct request to God to assist them to deal with that particular issue. If there is an impending decision that they need to conclude, make a request of God to affect that decision for the benefit of those that are called by God's Name.

- Give God thanks for holding the heart of your leaders in His hands. Pray and ask Him to turn their hearts in the direction that favours you and every believer under their authority.

## MY PROPHETIC DECLARATION

I declare that the kingdom is the Lord's, and He rules over the nations. He is called the God of the whole earth. Heavenly Father, You keep Your covenant and mercy with those who love You and observe Your commandments. Therefore, establish Your justice and correct every wicked manifestation of demonic powers in our leaders. I believe You have given me (call the name of the leader you are praying for) at such a time as this for my benefit, for the benefit of my family and for the benefit of my community and my Church. I declare that every decision that (insert their name once again) takes will favour me, my household and God's kingdom.

Lord God of heaven, Your Word declares that when the righteous are in authority, there is peace and the people rejoice. Therefore, I invoke Your mighty presence into the inner chamber of (insert name), so that as he/she ponders on the decisions to be made, You will turn his/her heart to favour me and my family. I declare that as the members of the legislature sit to deliberate on the future of this nation, Your presence will speak for every believer and that every decision taken will benefit the Church in Jesus' name.

Father I thank you for these ones (list every leader and every authority in your life) that you have placed over me as leaders. Pour Your Spirit of wisdom and grace upon them. Let them be for my benefit and for my increase. I thank you that they will not work against me but will work for me in Jesus' Name. They will not work against my destiny or that of my generation but they will work for our benefit in the name of Jesus.

# 8

## COPING WITH UNCERTAINTY

*My times are in your hands...*
Psalm 31:15a (AMP)

*And He changes the times and the seasons; He removes kings and raises up kings; He gives wisdom to the wise and knowledge to those who have understanding.*
Daniel 2:21 (NKJV)

*To everything there is a season, and a time for every matter or purpose under heaven:*
Ecclesiastes 3:1 (AMP)

*The Lord will open the heavens, the storehouse of his bounty, to send rain on your land in season and to bless all the work of your hands. You will lend to many nations but will borrow from none.*
Deuteronomy 28:12 (NIV)

## REFLECTION

One of my favourite songs by Fred Hammond says "the Lord holds the balance of our days." Yes, indeed He does, the Bible declares that He upholds all things by the Word of His power (Hebrews 1:3). I have always taken every opportunity to declare to the Lord that my times and my seasons are in His Hands! My times of joy, of sadness, of great victory and success and even the times when I seem to have failed....they are all in His Hands!

Gloria and William Gaither wrote the wonderful song:

*Because He lives I can face tomorrow,*
*Because He lives all fear is gone;*
*Because I know He holds the future*
*And life is worth the living just because He lives*

This is a song close to my heart and I love to sing it at every given opportunity. You may wonder why, well for me it emphasises God's Word and His grace for me to carry on no matter what. This brings a confirmation and a reassurance that whatever I am dealing with today; no matter how difficult or how life threatening it may be, "because He lives, I can face tomorrow." I can look forward with joy to the balance of my days here on earth without fear because Jesus lives!

Ecclesiastes 3:1 tells us there is an appointed time and season for everything under the sun. Also

Deuteronomy 28:12 reminds us that God will bless the work of our hands and that He will reward every effort we make - "in due season." So if you are reading this book and reckon your season is not what it should be, God has the power to change it. You may have been working tirelessly to achieve a set goal. God will prosper your efforts shortly in due season! Perhaps you have been sowing seeds and still looking out for a harvest - God will bring the increase in season. Be sure that you do not become weary in doing "good" as only those that endure till the end will receive the crown.

Do not let the trials of today cause you to give up on your tomorrow, don't permit the pain of today to cause you to lose out on the rejoicing of tomorrow. Do not let the difficulties of today cause you to give up on your bright and wonderful future! "For I know the plans I have for you," declares the LORD, "plans to prosper you and not to harm you, plans to give you hope and a future (Jeremiah 29:11)

Your future is better than you could ever imagine it to be! Your best days are ahead of you. The balance of your days is better and greater than the days you have lived so far! The Lord of hosts says "behold I do a new thing, now it shall spring forth..." (Isaiah 43:18 KJV). Because Jesus lives, every setback you have suffered will be restored and every force in heaven and on earth will work for your good in Jesus' Name!

## PRAYER POINTS

- Pray and decree stability concerning that confusing situation, that unknown circumstance that is plaguing your mind, that shaky job, that rickety relationship (name every uncertainty) pray that the all-knowing God who is your Father will cause it all to work out for your good according to His Word and purpose for your life in Jesus Name.

- Renounce all satanic powers, devices, imaginations and all attacks of the kingdom of darkness against your family. Give God praise concerning (name the situation) and declare that He holds the outcome of that situation in His hands.

- Give God thanks because your worst days are behind you and your best days are ahead of you, thank Him for the plans He has for you, plans to prosper you and give you an expected end and a glorious future!

- Ask your Father who holds all things in the palm of His Hands to turn your season around right now. Ask Him to change your circumstances according to His Divine plan.

- Prophesy that you will no longer apply maximal effort only to reap minimal results. Ask for an era of ease and a life of abundance.

- Contend against all insecurity, doubt and fear of the unknown that may hinder you from reaching or attaining your God-given goals, promises and purpose for your family.
- Lift up your hands and thank God that He is the one who holds your future in His hands. Thank Him because He is the one who embraces the balance of your days.

## MY PROPHETIC DECLARATION

I decree and declare that my times are in the Hands of God. My heavenly Father holds the balance of my days and He is working everything out for my good in Jesus' Name!

I declare in agreement with the song writer that because He lives, I can face tomorrow! Because He lives, all fear is gone! Because I am convinced and I know that God holds my future in His Hands, my life is worth living because He lives!

I declare that God prospers the work of my hands in season; He has flung open up the windows of heaven and caused rain to fall upon my seed in season. The Lord raises up and sets down kings for my sake and for my benefit.

The best days of my life are ahead of me, the worst days of my life are behind me, the best of my times and seasons are yet to come. God upholds me by the Word of His power; therefore I succeed in everything that my hand finds to do. I declare that every uncertain situation facing me (name the situation) works out for my good. Every condition in my life works out for my benefit, and it will be for gain and not for loss in Jesus' Name. From now on, I worry less because God is sorting out everything that concerns me. My peace, my gains from all efforts will bring me pleasure and much satisfaction. My expectancy for the future is great. I boldly declare that I have a favourable outcome in Jesus Name!

# 9

## ERASING LINES OF LIMITATION

*A certain woman of the wives of the sons of the prophets cried out to Elisha, saying, "Your servant my husband is dead, and you know that your servant feared the Lord. And the creditor is coming to take my two sons to be his slaves." So Elisha said to her, "What shall I do for you? Tell me, what do you have in the house?" And she said… nothing…but a jar of oil." Then he said, "Go, borrow vessels from everywhere, from all your neighbours – empty vessels; do not gather just a few…So she went from him and shut the door behind her and her sons, who brought the vessels to her; and she poured it out…when the vessels were full, she said to her son, "Bring me another vessel." And he said to her, "There is not another vessel." So the oil ceased.*
2 Kings 4:1-6 (NLT)


## REFLECTION

Oil is one of God's gifts to humanity. It is an indispensable substance widely used for multiple purposes. In the kitchen we rely on oil for cooking; whilst its use in cosmetics ensures the skin is moisturised. Indeed oil features in the medicine cabinet and of course at the pulpit for anointing. Let's not forget oil's pivotal role in lubrication of engines. In fact, in some places, as soon as the sun is set, the only source of light is the oil lamp. Oil is essential for everyday life and its benefits are tremendous.

Contrastingly, the absence of oil in our lives can lead to pain and suffering. If the oil of an engine runs out, damage is inevitable because oil eases things. It can also be the solution to various problems. The oil in 2 Kings 4:3-6 represents the oil of the Holy Spirit and it is symbolic of a gift to that widow. One good thing about God's gift is that it is enduring. Notice however, that the widow chose not to do anything with the little oil she had - probably because of fear. At times in life many people have only a minimalist expectation and are content with little oil. In other instances, there is presence of oil but evil powers may be leeching that oil in order to cause pain in one's life and undertakings. Friend, - this predicament calls for attention. Daniel 11:32(b) says *"….but the people who know their God shall prove themselves strong and shall stand firm and do exploits."* Many have the oil, but out of ignorance, feel it is too little to do anything, just like that widow. Hosea 4:6 says, *"My people are destroyed from lack of knowledge....*" The plan of God is to make you relevant and significant on earth. All too often we see gifted individuals with ideas, connections and opportunities but the problem is that they lack the ability to use their gifts appropriately.

Have you been on the same spot for a while as a result of limitations around you? Are you thinking of expansion? Hoping to buy your own property, start a business, pursuing a course, marrying, having children or some other progressive move? Don't delay – today is the day to arise and take that bold step of faith! Let your faith run ahead of your mentality. Take action before you are overtaken - make use of today, go on - do something before it is too late! Notice this - although the widow was willing to continue to pour the oil, when the vessels she had gathered were all filled and there was none left to be filled, the oil ceased. Why did the oil cease? The oil was flowing in proportion to her faith and ability. Friend, your capacity to progress in life and your level of passion for your vision will determine when the oil of success will stop. Always remember that God is your source and His resources are unlimited!

Believe in yourself - you are born to win and reign, you are not to be limited because we serve a limitless

God. No one that is born of God can be limited. Vince Lombardi said, "If you believe in yourself and have the courage, the determination, the dedication, the competitive drive and if you are willing to sacrifice the little things in life and pay the price for the things that are worthwhile, it can be done." Therefore, friend, be courageous and strong, become passionate from today and purpose in your heart to achieve. We must increase our mentality and ability because we serve a God who wants us to enlarge our horizon. Look into ways to improve yourself and remain current. The world is ever evolving so you must arise and make that necessary change to your calling and become relevant to your world. Be determined to overcome that limitation. What you see is what you can possess. Get more knowledge and do not be limited in your thinking. Think big and see big! ASK.

## PRAYER POINTS

- Earnestly renounce every wilderness experience of limitation and worthlessness to cease in your life and that of your family!

- Pray that your country will discover and explore all the natural resources given by God to the full benefit of the citizens to include you and your household.

- Boldly decree that your oil of ease will not cease but your jar of oil shall overflow with unlimited joy!

- Ask God to empower you to stretch your limits and increase your capacity whether through training or acquiring winning ideas to do the impossible.

- Ask the Lord to give you the knowledge and capability to use the little things in your life to make big impact in your community!

- Prophesy that you shall break forth into greatness and because of you generations will become blessed!

- Pray and prophesy that you will not neglect the gift of God in your life but will stir it up. Declare that wherever you turn with your gifts, you shall prosper!

## MY PROPHETIC DECLARATION

I decree and declare that every season of nothing is over in my life. I have received grace to operate under the anointing of ease. The oil of joy that makes achievement and attainment easy is upon me. I shall not be afraid to go into new territories.

I will arise and expand my capacity. My life shall yield abundant increase. I receive the wisdom for witty inventions and what to do to be relevant.

Though I was once despised but my days of struggling are over! For the Lord has turned my inadequacy for plenty. God's proof of grace is upon me to handle every situation in my life. I am clothed with strength to soar like an eagle and rise above every limiting situation. I will no longer live in shame for the Almighty is my God. He is my Redeemer who has called me back from nothing to something. I declare that my life will not be mediocre. My life will not be ordinary but extraordinary that I may become a blessing to my generations. The Revealer of mystery shall give me secret riches and treasures hidden in dark places. The heaven shall open up and pour out secrets of success and increase over me. I shall celebrate my triumph over the limits of yesterday. I triumphantly move towards the land of my overflowing joy. Nothing shall hinder me. I will not settle for any alternative plan. I am out to pursue the original plan, purpose and will of God for my life this year more than ever before. I am free from obstacles that hinder. I am free from limitations that prevent a full expression of my potential in Jesus Name!

# 10

## MAKE ME A SHOWCASE OF YOUR GLORY

*This beginning of signs Jesus did in Cana of Galilee, and manifested His glory; and His disciples believed in Him.*

John 2:11 (NKJV)

*Yes, there will be an abundance of flowers and singing and joy! The deserts will become as green as the mountains of Lebanon, as lovely as Mount Carmel or the Plain of Sharon. There the Lord will display His glory, the splendour of our God.*

Isaiah 35:2 (NLT)

*Then Moses said to Aaron, "This is what the Lord meant when He said, 'I will display my holiness through those who come near me.' I will display my glory before all the people.*

Leviticus 10:3 (NLT)

## REFLECTION

Have you noticed that every manufacturer needs a pedestal or prime spot where their finest products can be displayed? Whether they are designers of furniture, car makers, kitchen designers or fashion designers; a showroom or display unit is a common factor that enables manufacturers to exhibit their craft. Businesses allocate a huge quota of their budget to the aspect of display – ever noticed how intricate and breathtaking the dressing of some shop windows can be? Its all about attracting customers. I believe this is a practice learnt from the manufacturer of all things; our God who is the creator of all things. He crafted us and shows us off on the shop window of life!

God is always looking for an opportunity to display His awesome power and His glory on the earth. He makes a distinction between His people and the rest of the world by showing Himself strong in the lives of His chosen race. "I will make a distinction between my people and your people" declares the Lord. (Exodus 8:23; 9:4 and 11:7).

God will not be glorified if you are not resourceful; neither will He derive any pleasure from your life if you are unproductive. He will however undoubtedly get the glory from your situation when there is a turn around! Therefore do not be discouraged if you are dealing with a 'dry' spell' at the moment, it is an opportunity that God can use to showcase His authority as the great I Am, the One that opens doors that no one can shut. If you are looking for employment, it is a grand opportunity for Him to provide the best possible job for you! If you are dealing with barrenness, it is a grand stage for Him to show off His power and bless you with a quiver full of children! Are you a bachelor or disgruntled spinster? Have you been praying for what seems like an eternity for a life partner? God can surprise you with a husband or wife after His own heart that will make you the envy of the world. Whatever your challenge is, God rises up in such situations to make a distinction between you and the rest of the world.

The Bible records that we are His "chosen generation, a royal priesthood, a holy nation, a special people.... that you may proclaim the praises of Him who called you" (1 Pet 2:9 NKJV). We are made for signs and for wonders, therefore, our lives will be a spectacle of glory in our local environment and communities. When people come in contact with us and see God working in our lives, they will know and accept that indeed there is a God in Heaven, who rules in the affairs of man on the earth.

As you continue to serve the Lord and trust Him, He will display His splendour and power in your life. When He reveals His glory in your life, everything will become beautiful and wonderful (Isaiah 35:2). Your life will be the place where He displays His greatness and His Omnipotence. In fact I will go further and say that your life will be the showroom for His power and His glory! Now do you see that you are truly His Masterpiece?

## PRAYER POINTS

- Lord God Almighty, I release my life and my circumstances into Your hands, to be used as a display of Your power and glory in all the earth.

- Lord, let my life be the showroom for Your glory; make my home a showcase of Your greatness. Let Your glory make me and my family the envy of nations in the Name of Jesus.

- Lord, let my present circumstances (name the situation you are in) be the perfect stage for You to display Your strength. Let all those around me see that there is a God in heaven and that You are at work in my life.

- I decree that I shall impart in an outstanding and sensational manner excellence into the lives of those around me.

- I prophesy that that God will make me an eternal excellency and a joy of many generations. I will serve my generation and my service will count for time and eternity.

- Lord Jesus, from the platform of faith, I decree that You will make a distinction between my family and the rest of my community, use our home, our lives, our health, our finances as the centre stage to show forth the mighty wonders of Your power.

- Cause me to dwell in peace and in safety Oh Lord and judge those around me who mock me and attempt to make my life difficult, let them recognise and see that You Oh Lord are at work in my life.

## MY PROPHETIC DECLARATION

I declare that my life is the showcase of the Lord's glory and His power. I decree and declare that my present situation is the very stage that the Lord will use to display His mighty power in all the earth. I declare that my life is beautified by the glory of the Lord which has risen over me.

I am a chosen generation of the Lord; I am His royal priesthood and a holy nation, chosen to display and show forth His glory in this 21st century and in this age. I am chosen as His display centre to cause men to see and recognise that there is a God in heaven who is at work in my life. My family is the pedestal point of the Lord; my children and I are for signs and wonders in this generation. My generation and I are an eternal, excellent epitome of joy. Henceforth all generations and nations shall call me blessed. I will serve my generation as David served his generation in a distinguished and unparalleled way. Because I am a showcase of God's work, nations shall seek me and gravitate towards me from far and near for counsel, support and comfort. For I have the unction to do common things in an uncommon way.

The Lord flaunts His splendour in my finances; He displays His power in my body and in my health. He demonstrates His power in my womb/my loins. He exhibits His power in my ministry; He parades His power in my job in the mighty Name of Jesus. I am a showcase of the Lord in every aspect of my very being! Halleluyah!

# RESTORATION

*I will seek what was lost and bring back what was driven away, bind up the broken and strengthen what was sick...*

Ezekiel 34:16a (NKJV)

*So I will restore to you the years that the swarming locust has eaten, The crawling locust, The consuming locust, And the chewing locust, My great army which I sent among you.*

Joel 2:25 (NKJV)

*This is what the LORD says: '...I will restore the fortunes of Jacob's tents and have compassion on his dwellings...'*

Jeremiah 30:18a (NIV)

## REFLECTION

We have all suffered loss at one point or another. I am sure everyone reading this book can easily recall something or someone that they have lost suddenly! Perhaps the enemy has been holding onto something precious of yours for a while? When the unexpected happens such as a sudden loss, it is the time we are most inclined to ask the question, why? Why me?

The occurrence of unexpected loss is not a strange thing, the Bible says "No temptation has seized you except what is common to man. And God is faithful; He will not let you be tempted beyond what you can bear. But when you are tempted, he will also provide a way out so that you can stand up under it" (1 Corinthians 12:13 NIV). There is nothing new under the sun and I can tell you that you are not the first person (nor will you be the last) to have to deal with the loss of someone or something.

God is in the business of restoration, He will bring back whatever you have lost. He will mend whatever has been broken. God will heal and perfect everything that is not at ease according to His Word. Have you had a major financial loss in hard times? God will rcstore it all but you have to be optimistic. Helen Keller counselled, "Optimism is the faith that leads to achievement."

Never forget that whenever you are faced with any sort of loss, the Holy Spirit will rise to your defence. Let's look at Isaiah 59:19 in a different light. Theologians have stated that the original manuscript of this verse had no actual punctuations so let us move the punctuation in the verse and see what it would mean .... *"When the enemy comes in, the Spirit of the Lord will lift up a standard against him like a flood!"* (Rendition is author's). So whenever you are faced with an unusual dilemma, be rest assured that the Spirit of the Lord will rise like a flood and drown out the attack! The Spirit will lift the standard, i.e. He will raise the bar....literally indicating to the enemy that this is too high, too much for you to touch or destroy! Halleluyah! The devil may try repeatedly but each time, the Spirit of the Lord will raise a standard against him. God did it for King David in spite of losing everything to the enemy in 1 Samuel 30. It's so amazing that David was not only restored to his previous status but experienced a two-fold effect! In the final analysis, be encouraged that whatever you have lost to the enemy, you will recover all and be restored in Jesus Name!

## PRAYER POINTS

- Command the enemy who is threatening to pursue, overtake and spoil you to drown in the red sea of God's wrath and displeasure before your eyes.

- Decree that you are free from every curse of loss

that operates in people's lives. Prophesy that you are free from the dictates, thoughts and manifestations of sorrow and grief.

- Place a demand on God that there be a reinstatement in your life, a restoration of that which you have lost.

- Ask for compassion from the Lord such that will result in your fortunes being restored no matter the reason why or how you have lost them.

- (For those who have lost a loved one) Ask for the grace and the mercy of God to help you to deal with the situation of the loss in Jesus Name. Ask for God's peace to flood your heart.

- Pray and ask for gladness to replace your sorrow, shame, pain and hurt. Plead the mercy of God for restoration of everything the locust has eaten.

- Ask God to award you an open heaven, open doors, multiple opportunities, wisdom, good food, great favour and, sound health all of which will befit the life of a restored child of God!

## MY PROPHETIC DECLARATION

God of restoration, I thank you for the gift of life and the opportunity to be restored. I decree and declare that every loss I have suffered is restored in Jesus' Name. I decree every sudden occurrence in my life that has caused me pain and misery to be turned around speedily in the Name of Jesus. I call forth and declare that there will be a restoration in my life in the Name of Jesus.

I decree that those who want my downfall shall be confounded and put to shame. They shall be turned back from their plan against me and my family and brought to confusion. Destruction shall come upon them unawares and they shall fall into the pit they dug in Jesus' Name! Every sorrow and defeat in my life ends today for the angel of the Lord shall pursue and overtake them to recover what they have stolen from me. I declare that my life shall not be a wasteland in lack and loss; instead it shall be etched in gold on the sands of my time, and upon the granite of eternity shall it recorded for the times to come.

I am completely free in Spirit, soul and body. I am free from every disease that was commonplace with me in the past. I am free from every sickness that seems to be rampant in my family. None of them shall be found in my family. I represent a breaking away from the past. I am spending my days in prosperity and my years in pleasure. I boldly declare that I am free from all loss and all other destructive emotions. I shall eat in plenty and be satisfied.

# 12

## THE STORM IS OVER NOW!

*And He arose and rebuked the wind and said to the sea, Hush now! Be still (muzzled)! And the wind ceased (sank to rest as if exhausted by its beating) and there was [immediately] a great calm (a perfect peacefulness).*

Mark 4:39 (AMP)

*Do not fret or have any anxiety about anything, but in every circumstance and in everything, by prayer and petition (definite requests), with thanksgiving, continue to make your wants known to God. And God's peace [shall be yours, that tranquil state of a soul assured of its salvation through Christ, and so fearing nothing from God and being content with its earthly lot of whatever sort that is, that peace] which transcends all understanding shall garrison and mount guard over your hearts and minds in Christ Jesus.*

Philippians 4:6-7 (AMP)

*But after long abstinence from food, then Paul stood in the midst of them and said, 'Men, you should have listened to me, and not have sailed from Crete and incurred this disaster and loss. And now I urge you to take heart, for there will be no loss of life among you, but only of the ship.*

Acts 27:21-22 (NKJV)

## REFLECTION

The devil is described as a 'roaring lion' going to and fro, seeking whom he may devour; he is a master con artiste and is very good at blowing situations out of proportion or giving you the impression that your circumstance is going to bury you. Notice that he can only 'act as a roaring lion' but he is not one! Jesus is the authentic Lion of the tribe of Judah and next to Him – the devil is a mere pussy cat! The enemy will create confusion around you and sometimes throw things at you that will threaten your peace of mind and comfort.

At such critical times, when your circumstances seem to be screaming insancly at you; just take a step back and say "hush" to everything negative around you, silencing every voice like your Master Jesus saying "peace be still". The Bible tells us to "follow after Christ" and since Jesus directly addressed turbulence around Him to 'be still', we need to do the same. There is no room for the faint hearted in today's Christian world. The Bible tells us that "from the days of John the Baptist until now the kingdom of heaven suffers violence, and the violent take it by force (Matthew 11:12 NKJV).

Sometimes God allows us to go through certain things to test our faith. Instead of being fearful, be cheerful and trust God that the storm you are passing through is temporary and that the siege will soon be over. In the account of the Shipwreck in the book of Acts chapter 27, the Bible says while people were giving up hope, Paul was praying about their hopeless nightmare. He encouraged his colleagues and shouted in the midst of the noise of the raging storm that they should not lose heart because no life will be lost among them - only the ship would suffer damage. As declared by Paul according to God's promise, the siege came to pass and no life was lost.

If you want peace, you are going to have to do something about it. If you want calm in your life, it is not going to come to you by wishing for it, you are going to have to command it to happen. You will need to point at the situation and command it to hush! There is also a time when you are so filled with the Word of God that simply walking into a situation causes the storm or turbulence to immediately cease. "And when they got into the boat, the wind ceased" (Matthew 14:32 AMP). The verse is speaking about Peter who was with the

Word of God (Jesus) barefooted on water and as soon as they stepped into the boat which was being tossed about, the wind stopped! God indeed keeps us in perfect peace, those whose minds are stayed on Him, stayed on His Word!

Another option for dealing with turbulent times is simply taking everything that is causing all the trouble around you, and placing them at the feet of Jesus, Philippians 4:6 tells us not to fret about anything but deal with them by praying and petitioning God. When you do this, then peace, and I mean indescribable peace will mount a guard and garrison your heart (like an army) and ensure that no trouble gets through to your heart any more.

## PRAYER POINTS

- Make a list of the situations that are causing turbulence around you, talk to God about every one of them, lay them at His feet. Declare that you will hold on to your faith in God whatever the tempest that blows your way.

- Plead the mercy of God upon the situation you are faced with. Specifically tell God what you want Him to do concerning each of those situations.

- Pray and order automatic calm against every satanic storm that has become a barrier to your advancement and destiny.

- Pray and charge  every terror of the day and of the night to be totally silent before you

-  Make an instant declaration and pray for the peace of your Country so that you may live tranquil and quiet lives.

- Prophesy and decree that every storm of life that rises up against you shall sink for your sake in Jesus' Name!

- Request absolute calm in every area of storm in your finances, in your home, in your health, in your job, in your family, in the lives of your children and so on. Boldly declare and believe that the storm is over!

## MY PROPHETIC DECLARATION

I decree and declare that nothing shall cause me to lose my peace in the Name of Jesus. I speak peace to every facet of my life, I speak peace to my family, I speak peace to my children and I speak peace to my career. I say to that situation (call the situation you are dealing with by name) hush in Jesus' victorious name! I triumph over this storm and its wickedness and perverseness. The storm may rage but I am confident and declare that no life shall be lost in my family in Jesus Name! I march on triumphantly out of this raging storm, without looking backwards or sideways, rather I focus upon God's goals for my life.

I shall celebrate my triumph over every raging storm. Every opposition, rocky terrain, mountains and other distractions, shall be trodden upon, as I triumphantly move towards the land of my peace. No one shall be able to resist or stop me from entering into the land of God's promises for me this year. I will not lose heart but I am rising to take my place and position. I will triumph, sing and shout for joy at the works of God's hands upon my life and the lives of my loved ones in Jesus' Name.

I declare that I will keep my mind stayed on Jesus and on His Word. I bring everything to Him in prayer and supplication; therefore peace has mounted a garrison, and is keeping watch over my heart in the Name of Jesus. I have the peace of God that surpasses all human understanding and I boldly declare this day that the storm is over and I walk in serenity and dwell in absolute peace.

## VICTORY OVER FEAR

*There shall no man be able to stand before you; the Lord your God shall lay the fear and the dread of you upon all the land that you shall tread, as He has said to you.*

Deuteronomy 11:25 (AMP)

*Fear not [there is nothing to fear], for I am with you; do not look around you in terror and be dismayed, for I am your God. I will strengthen and harden you to difficulties, yes, I will help you; yes, I will hold you up and retain you with My [victorious] right hand of rightness and justice*

Isaiah 41:10 (AMP)

*Even though I walk through the valley of the shadow of death, I will fear no evil, for You are with me; Your rod and Your staff, they comfort me.*

Psalm 23:4 (KJV)

## REFLECTION

The Word of God repeatedly records the injunction

"fear not" or "do not be afraid". It actually appears 365 times in the Bible! Yes, that's correct one for each day of the year! Why do you think this phrase is used more frequently than any other phrase in the Bible? Perhaps God knows that fear will rob you of His promises for your life. Indeed just as much as faith will activate the promises of God in your life, fear will activate the desire of the enemy over you.

In order for anything to grow an optimum environment is required. For instance mould needs moisture and ambient temperature to grow and breed. Bacteria also need a certain type of environment in order to multiply and do their damage effectively. The enemy is no different - they need the right type of atmosphere in order to grow and breed in your life and cause you damage. One of the perfect conditions that make your life suitable for the devil to operate is fear! Is there any wonder then that God tells us 365 times, "fear not!" Banishing fear from your life is one way you can exclude the working of the devil in your life. Remember the story of Job? He lived in the fear that his children might sin and bring calamity into his life. According to Job's own testimony, calamity, the very thing he feared the most came upon him swiftly - "What I always feared has happened to me. What I dreaded has come true" (Job 3:25 NLT).

Jesus said He came to destroy the works of the enemy, "The reason the Son of God was made manifest (visible) was to undo (destroy, loosen, and dissolve) the works the devil [has done]. (1 John 3:8b AMP). Jesus came to destroy and banish fear from your life; He has freely given of His Spirit which is a Spirit of power, love and a sound mind. There is absolutely no reason why you should let fear rule in any area of your life. Fear is detestable and not to be tolerated or entertained in the life of the believer. Fear of the past, present or future should have no place in your life! "Do not be terrified by them, for the LORD your God, who is among you, is a great and awesome God" (Deuteronomy 7:21).

The fact that God says "fear not" means that He has fore knowledge that there may be reasons for you to fear. He has gone ahead and knows that impending difficult circumstance that you will face that might cause you to become fearful. Despite these facts, God states emphatically "....I will strengthen and harden you to difficulties, yes, I will help you; yes, I will hold you up and retain you with My [victorious] right hand of rightness and justice" (Isaiah 41:10 AMP).

Are you faced with a frightening prospect that has gripped you with fear, is it regarding your home, employment, ministry or something else? It really does not matter what it is – the answer is the same, once again fear not. God has promised that He will lay the dread and fear of you upon everybody you have to deal with! You are too hot to handle for the devil and all of his cohorts!

## PRAYER POINTS

- Lord Jesus, turn to me and be gracious to me, for I am fearful and in constant dread. Free me from every torment of the enemy and take away all my fear in Jesus' Name!

- My Lord and my God fill my life with fearlessness; let your boldness overwhelm me in every circumstance in Jesus' Name.

- Lord God Almighty, let them that desire to do me harm, and those whose activities cause me to fear, begin to experience the dread and fear of me coming upon them in Jesus Name.

- My Lord and my God let the dread of my family, that of my children come upon everyone and everything that seeks to do us harm in Jesus Name.

- Victorious Lord of heaven, deliver me from the constant fear and dread of death.

- My Lord God, when situations rise up against me, let the boldness of Your Holy Spirit rise up on the inside of me, to declare that I shall not fear because You are the Strength of my life.
- From today, I renounce every spirit of fear. I renounce panic attacks. I decree and declare that I will no longer be afraid. I am free from the bondage of fear and I have total peace in Jesus Name.

## MY PROPHETIC DECLARATION

I decree that God Almighty is my salvation; He is my strength and my song. Therefore, I will not be afraid of sudden disaster. For the Lord God is my hope. My going out shall be safe. My coming in shall be secured. I declare that the rod of the wicked shall not fall upon my lot. As mountains surround Jerusalem, so the Lord surrounds me with His love. The Lord God Almighty is my Redeemer, and my Deliverer. He is my Refuge and my Strong Tower. He is my Confidence and my Assurance that I will be preserved despite everything that I go through in the Name of Jesus.

I declare that the Lord strengthens me and hardens me through difficulties. He is my Help, my Shield and my Defence. I am convinced that even in this situation that is causing me to have panic attacks (name the situation you are dealing with); I will experience the courage and the victory of the Lord in the mighty Name of Jesus.

I am enjoying the goodness of the Lord in the land of the living and I have no more fear of tomorrow for He that holds tomorrow is my guide. I rebuke every spirit that wants to shorten my days and years to desist. I rebuke every spirit that opposes the enactment and fulfilment of my God given destiny. Avenues and channels of blessings and favour are multiplied to me. I declare that I have been set free from everything the devil has set up as fear to my profiting this year and beyond. This is my year of definition and I shall be even more outstanding than former years. I overcome fear by the Blood of the Lamb. No more fear of tomorrow! No more fear of financial and emotional pressure for the Lord is my strength and defence. Victory is mine from today in Jesus' Name!

# 14

## VICTORY ON EVERY SIDE

*If anyone does attack you, it will not be my doing; whoever attacks you will surrender to you*
                                                Isaiah 54:15 (NIV)

*No weapon that is formed against thee shall prosper; and every tongue that shall rise against thee in judgment thou shalt condemn...*
                                                Isaiah 54:17 (KJV)

*The LORD will conquer your enemies when they attack you. They will attack you from one direction, but they will scatter from you in seven*
                                                Deuteronomy 28:7 (NLT)

## REFLECTION

The Word of God tells us to anticipate attack whilst we remain on the earth. Jesus says "*...In the world you have tribulation and trials and distress and frustration; but be of good cheer [take courage; be confident, certain, undaunted]! For I have overcome* *the world. [I have deprived it of power to harm you and have conquered it for you.] (John16:33 AMP).* Isn't that simply wonderful! Yes there will be trials and men will rise up and attack you, but the Master says He has deprived them all of the power to harm you!

Have a look at the scriptures listed above and thoroughly digest them. I want you to read them in the context of the battle you are faced with presently. Appropriate them specifically to the battles or even individuals who have wickedly chosen to attack you whether physically or spiritually. You do have the strength to crush that army that has risen up against you. Yes, you have the strength to scale the wall and penetrate the barricade that they have placed in front of you. The Bible says everyone who attacks you will surely have to surrender to you because the Most High God is your hiding place, your dwelling place, your place of refuge, your strong tower that can not be breached! Therefore, your safekeeping is guaranteed when you are under the attack of the enemy. Yes, they may try to harm you but you are safe in the arms of your Father.

When you have Jesus as your fortress, whosoever gathers against your goodness, will fall for your sake. They will be made to flee from you scattered in several directions because the terror of the Lord your God will overtake them and utterly defeat and destroy them! Do not let the attack or attacker cause you to lose heart nor allow any scheming of the enemy cause you to lose sleep. As surely as God lives, they will be scattered, defeated and destroyed. As Moses said to the children of Israel, "the Egyptians (enemies) you see today, you will see them no more... stand back and see the Salvation of the Lord!"

## PRAYER POINTS

- Call on the Mighty God of all the earth, Champion of the armies of Israel, to arise and let all your enemies be scattered and flee from you in fear.

- Decree and declare that no weapon formed against you and your family shall prosper. Prophesy that even if it has been formed it shall not work but backfire against the evildoer.

- Pray and ask the Lord for strength to overcome every obstacle placed in front of you. Pray for strength and wisdom to defeat every enemy and army that has gathered against you

- Prophesy that since you are more than conquerors in Christ; no attack, offence, trial, challenge, hardship or persecution shall hinder you from putting your hope in God.

- Pray and bind every power engineered by the enemy against you and all that is yours. Take authority over their powers and declare them subdued and captive in the Mighty Name of Jesus.

- Prophesy and declare that since you have been given the authority over all the power of the enemy, nothing shall by any means hurt you.

- Pray that those who secretly seek your hurt, your downfall, and your defeat will be exposed and brought to justice.

## MY PROPHETIC DECLARATION

I declare according to Psalm 90 that I dwell in the shelter of the Most High; I rest in the shadow of the Almighty. I say of the LORD, "He is my refuge and my fortress, my God, in whom I trust." Surely He will save me from the fowler's snare and from the deadly pestilence. He will cover me with His feathers, and under His wings I will always find refuge; His faithfulness will be my shield and rampart. I will not fear the terror of night, nor the arrow that flies by day, nor the pestilence that stalks in the darkness, nor the plague that destroys at midday. A thousand may fall at my side, ten thousand at my right hand, but it will not come near me. I will only observe with my eyes and see the punishment of the wicked. I have made the Most High my dwelling place even the Lord, as my refuge, therefore no harm will befall me, no disaster will come near my tent. The Lord will command His angels concerning me to guard me in all my ways; they will lift me up in their hands, so that I will not strike my foot against a stone. I will tread upon the lion and the cobra; I will trample the great lion and the serpent. Because I love the Lord, He will rescue me; He will protect me, because I acknowledge His Name. I will call upon Him, and He will answer me; He will be with me in trouble, He will deliver me and honour me. With long life will He satisfy me and show me His salvation.

I declare that the Lord is my strength and shield, He is my help and defence; the Lord is my courage and the pride of my song. Whosoever rises against me; shall be smitten before me. They shall be dashed into pieces and be drowned in the sea of God's wrath. I decree that the rod of the wicked shall not fall upon my household. Every tree my heavenly Father has not planted, I uproot and destroy. I will not be ashamed and my enemies will never triumph over me in Jesus' Name!

## THRIVING IN A TIME LIKE THIS

*Now there was no bread in all the land; for the famine was very severe... So when the money failed in the land of Egypt and in the land of Canaan, all the Egyptians came to Joseph and said, "Give us bread, for why should we die in your presence? For the money has failed."*

Genesis 47:13,15 (NKJV)

*Thou shalt also decree a thing, and it shall be established unto thee: and the light shall shine upon thy ways. When men are cast down, then thou shalt say, There is lifting up...;*

Job 22:28-29a (KJV)

*Do not call conspiracy everything that these people call conspiracy; do not fear what they fear, and do not dread it.*

Isaiah 8:12 (NIV)

**REFLECTION**

Isn't it amazing how things have taken a downturn in our world today? We should not be ignorant of the fact that what the world calls recession is actually famine. Famine attacks a nation or person whom God's hands have gone against. Please note that recession is the complete opposite to progression – when God's hand is absent in your life you will recess – let us not be deceived! Going back to the Bible days, it was recorded in Genesis 47:13-15 that the famine worsened to the extent that even their money ran out! Just as currencies all around the world are loosing their values in a time like this, their money also lost its value! However, in the same place where there was famine, Joseph and his people survived because of the promises of God concerning them. As God's chosen people, we ought to change our own vocabulary and align it to the level of God's Word. Contrary to what you may be going through in a time like this, remember that what you say is powerful therefore, spcak positively.

It is apparent that the state of the world today can often be discouraging, nevertheless, let not your heart be troubled for in our tongue lies the power of life and death. When we speak, we are literally commanding everything around us; in fact we are commanding all of creation. The Bible tells us "life and death are in the power of the tongue" (Prov.

18:21). Another version states, "The tongue can bring death or life" (NLT). So when things around you seem to take a downturn - as they are right now across the globe, whether in your life or in the life of those around you, do not say "recession" like every body else, instead say it is booming! Say abundance! Say there are plenty of possessions for you! Say there is lifting up; because what you say, what you decree, will be established! As Joseph and his people thrived in a time like this in Egypt, you too will thrive because we serve the same living God. Where there is famine or as they call it "recession" you will be nourished and thrive in the same place in Jesus Name!

Job 22:29 suggests that when you speak, it is like pointing a flash light upon the situation you are speaking about. It is empowering the situation you are speaking about to move in the direction you "speak it" or command it to go. The light and power of your words will direct your situation irrespective of what is happening around you. Conversely, your situation can go in the exact opposite direction if you command it to!

Do you know something else? God's word commands us not to make the same pronouncements as the world around us. His word commands us not to fear what the world fears! He clearly says, do not say there is a recession, when the world says there is a recession; do not live in fear of a famine because they live in fear of a famine. Do not dread what they fear! In order to live and rise above our situations when things take a slump, in a time like this, we must speak God's Word in order to see it come to pass because you will not possess it until you actually say/ see it. We must speak progression and promotion in the midst of a recession around us! Remember, our God is known as Jehovah Jireh, meaning the Lord will provide because He is all-sufficient and He owns everything. Therefore, ASK!

## PRAYER POINTS

- Rebuke the spirit of lack and reject anything that falls short of multiplication in your life. Ask him to multiply all that you have for good.

- Pray and petition God to multiply your income, your seed sown and to multiply your strength in challenging times.

- Pray and ask Jehovah Jireh that your daily bread and that of your family will be continually supplied in a time like this.

- Pray and ask the All-Sufficient Father to surround you and your family with His own presence and that the turmoil outside in the world will not break into your family.

- Pray and ask that the turmoil in the financial world will not penetrate into your finances and the finances of your family. Decree that money will not fail you.

- Pray that in the midst of famine in the land, you will sow and reap a bountiful harvest. Decree that harvest time shall not cease in your home.

- Confidently declare that you will not borrow, you will never lack good things and that God will supply all your needs according to His riches!

## MY PROPHETIC DECLARATION

Almighty God, All-Sufficient Father, Jehovah Jireh, I declare that You are the Eternal Rock of Ages. You are He who controls the entire universe, and You have granted me the ability to control my tongue, to speak life to my every situation. Thank you for the ability to say only the right things, to speak only words of life to my circumstance. I decree that in a time like this, as for me and my family there is harvest in Jesus' Name. I decree that in the midst of job losses, repossession of properties, selling of investments for food, business losses, and excessive borrowing for daily sustenance (mention any other areas of scarcity), for me and my family there is abundance in Jesus' Name.

I declare that in the midst of property losses and repossessions, I acquire more and more equity in Jesus Name! All that I do is yielding unto me their full strength. The seeds I am sowing in tears are being multiplied exceedingly back to me in unusual measures and from uncommon sources. I have no lack in all I do for I have all things and abound. I am blessed and experiencing multiplication in all my returns. I enjoy the compassion of the Lord and this keeps evil things from multiplying in my life. The numbers of those who despise my righteous cause are diminishing while those who are willing to collaborate for my welfare and well-being are multiplying continuously. I know the lions sometimes go hungry, but I believe that those who trust in the Lord will never lack any good thing. Therefore I declare that... (Open your mouth and begin to make bold and progressive declarations concerning the issues in your life, your destiny, your family, your children, and your job e.t.c.) in Jesus' Name.

## BLESSED BEYOND THE CURSE

*Our fathers sinned and are no more, But we bear their iniquities.*

Lamentations 5:7 (NKJV)

*In those days they shall say no more: 'The fathers have eaten sour grapes, and the children's teeth are set on edge.' But every one shall die for his own iniquity; every man who eats the sour grapes, his teeth shall be set on edge.*

Jeremiah 31:29-30 (NKJV)

*Christ redeemed us from the curse of the law by becoming a curse for us, for it is written: "Cursed is everyone who is hung on a tree.*

Galatians 3:13 (NIV)

## REFLECTION

In the introductory section of this book, I talked about certain occurrences in my family which I later recognised as a trend. Laura's story also indicated a trend of unbroken curses. However, those evil trends have been destroyed by the power in the Name of Jesus. I resolved that enough was enough and followed divine directions with a regime of fasting and prayer to eliminate the evil pattern. My entire family are now enjoying the benefit of the decision I took at that time through the help of God. In the first volume of this book, I mentioned that we must not just rollover and accept "this is a pattern in my family or this is my destiny" or just overlook or even ignore evil trends or patterns of tragedies, stagnation and failure. The Bible says, "For Zion's sake I will not hold My peace..." (Isaiah 62:1). This tells us that if everyone around you has signed up to 'a vow of silence' whilst the devil is on the loose; then you should not, because you have to pray continually without resting, trusting God that you and your family will be delivered from the mouth of the enemy. Friend, don't live your life in mediocrity. Refuse to rest until you have feasted on that prey who has purposed to cause you nothing but grief!

Perhaps you come from a family like mine, with the occurrence of premature deaths after the exit of your father or a head of the family as some may say. Or maybe you come from a family with patterns of abnormal delay prior to marriage, disfavour, divorce, strange and unprovoked complications with conception and pregnancy. Perhaps your lineage has a family history of sickness, failure at the brink of breakthrough or some other really devastating trend. Then it is time to stand up and declare: enough! For God's Word says every record against us and every charge; every contract entered into by us or on our behalf whether by our parents or siblings has been discharged! How? Christ took it all away and nailed them to the cross over 2000 years ago! (Colossians 2:14). So as long as I have accepted Christ and His finished work upon the Cross, every negative contract, evil pronouncement by anyone and every curse against my life, has been nailed to the Cross and taken away from me for ever.

Friend isn't it just gracious to know that God has also declared concerning you that there is no enchantment, or evil pronouncement against you that will work and certainly no divination against your family will succeed. However, it will now be said of you and your loved ones, see the wonders God has done! (Numbers 23:23 emphasis mine)  I meditated and considered this scripture as I went before God to intercede on behalf of my family. Another scripture that came to mind reads…"Like a fluttering sparrow or a darting swallow, an undeserved curse does not come to rest" (Proverb 26:2 NIV). If you have not committed any treachery and you have not entered into a contract with the kingdom of the enemy, then you do not deserve to receive any repercussion for such. If by some error of yours or due to your ignorance you have entered into a negative contract, the Word of God says "Can plunder be taken from warriors, or captives rescued from the fierce? But this is what the LORD says: "Yes, captives will be taken from warriors, and plunder retrieved from the fierce; I will contend with those who contend with you and your children I will save." (Isaiah 49:24-25 NIV)

Galatians chapter 3:13 clearly states that Jesus became a curse for us in order that we might be redeemed from every curse. So no matter how or why a curse has come into your life, Christ has redeemed you from it all at the Cross of Calvary! However, do not remain quiet but ASK!

## PRAYER POINTS

- Go before your heavenly Father in prayer and remind Him of His Word concerning every curse afflicting your life and your family. Neutralise and reverse every evil word pronounced upon your life by anyone.

- Decree and declare that no curse without cause will work against you or your family and that every contract you know nothing about will not hold you down or affect you.

- Pray and break every curse of premature deaths, failure at the brink of breakthrough, financial hardship, marital failure, inherited sickness (mention the name) that has persisted so far in your life and your family. Plead the Blood of Jesus upon all of these.

- Pray that the Lord will take up your battles and fight for you and your family. Pray that your children will be saved from the effect of every curse. Decree that your children will not live in bondage of any sort.

- Pray that every outstanding code, evil handwriting of the enemy and wicked ordinances standing against you and against your family be erased by the Blood of Jesus.

- Pray that no divination or enchantment against you or your family will succeed. Prophesy that you will walk in the covenant blessings of God.

- Pray that no plan or desire of the kingdom of darkness over your life will see the light of day. Prophesy blessings, favour in the sight of the enemy, perfect health, prosperity, peace and security to come upon you and your family.

## MY PROPHETIC DECLARATION

I decree that Christ has redeemed me and my loved ones from the curse of the law because He was made a curse for us. Therefore, in righteousness I shall be established. Oppression and every effect of evil incantations shall be far from me. Every wicked cloud over my life is hereby lifted. Every curse and evil pronouncement over my life is broken in Jesus' Name! Every contract entered into by my parents or family members will have no impact upon me. I stand upon the Blood of Jesus and I cancel every pact concerning my loved ones in the kingdom of darkness! I overturn and overthrow every demonic treaty with death and the grave! In the name that is above every other name, I undo every work of the kingdom of darkness in my life and in my family in Jesus' Name. Never again will anyone call me forsaken, nor shall my home be termed as desolate. But I shall be called the delight of the Most High God. My life shall be free of grief and will be peaceful in Jesus Name!

By the reason of the anointing, I decree and declare that every evil handwriting against my family has been nailed to the cross and taken away. I shall not die for the sins of others nor bear the curse of any known or unknown relative, for I have been redeemed from the curse of the law because Jesus became a curse for me to set me free. I declare that

I am delivered from every stronghold that has held me bound. Blessed be the Lord God of heaven, who has not given me as prey to their teeth. I declare that I have escaped from every generational curse like a bird from the snare of the fowler; the trap of wicked curses have been broken and I have escaped to be set free for life in Christ in Jesus' Name!

## MASTERING COMPLACENCY

*So, because you are lukewarm – neither hot nor cold – I am about to spit you out of my mouth.*
Revelation 3:16 (NIV)

*That is why I would remind you to stir up (rekindle the embers of, fan the flame of, and keep burning) the [gracious] gift of God, [the inner fire] that is in you by means of the laying on of my hands [with those of the elders at your ordination]*
2 Timothy 1:6 (AMP)

*But you, beloved, build yourselves up [founded] on your most holy faith [make progress, rise like an edifice higher and higher], praying in the Holy Spirit…*
Jude 1:20 (AMP)

**REFLECTION**
They say that everyone goes through a dry patch, otherwise known as a period of un-productivity. Footballers and their fans often call it a blip; I however, will call it a period of complacency. We

all get to a point when other things crowd into our prayer and Bible study time. Sometimes we are so overwhelmed with the pressures of daily activities that we say to ourselves, "I need a vacation". At that time we inadvertently drift away from our close relationship with God; as believers we cannot afford such times. The Bible tells us in 1 Peter 5:8 to be on our guard, and not let things slip. "Be well balanced (temperate, sober of mind), be vigilant and cautious at all times; for that enemy of yours, the devil, roams around like a lion roaring [in fierce hunger], seeking someone to seize upon and devour."

When believers stray from the covering of God's cloak they become vulnerable to the attack of the enemy. Immediately, that "sin that easily besets us" (Hebrew 12:1) tends to creep in. God does not like lukewarm service and warns against complacency. He encourages us to *keep* the fire burning, but the fire is not going to stay burning by itself. You must be prepared to take positive action and key into the Word of God according to 2 Timothy 1:6 "...fan into flames the spiritual gift God gave you when I laid my hands on you." If you fail to do this, you run the risk of losing the fire completely, and are in danger of becoming just like the Church in Laodicea referred to in Revelation 3:14-6.

Satan's strategy is to get God's people overwhelmed with worldly issues, his intent being to choke out the Word of God in your life and throw your relationship with God into disarray; then he pounces and attacks you when you least expect it. Do not give room to his distractive tactics and do not be ignorant of the devil's devices (2 Corinthians 2:12).

I am sure I am not wrong in assuming that every believer experiences periods of lapse in their daily walk with God. When I personally feel complacency setting in and I begin to struggle with my prayer life or studying the Word, I do exactly what the Apostle Jude encourages us to do in the book of Jude 1:20, I build up myself in my most holy faith, praying in tongues. The ability to pray in tongues is a useful tool in dealing with complacency in prayer. It is a heavenly language that only God understands, it confounds the devil and his cohorts and that confusion sets them into flight! When prayer becomes hard work or you cannot think of anything to pray about, just open your mouth and let that heavenly language pour out. You can never pray wrong when you are praying in the Spirit. I encourage you to seek the gift of praying in tongues if you do not already have it, you will find it to be a very valuable tool in your walk of faith.

## PRAYER POINTS

- Pray and renounce every spirit of lukewarm ness and spiritual complacency. Ask God to give you a heart that will not compromise your worship for Him.

- Ask God to destroy every 'fire extinguisher' in your life. Pray and ask God to help you fan into flame the gift that He has deposited in you.

- Pray and decree that all desires shall be granted in His Presence whenever you approach God in prayers.

- Pray saying 'Lord let my circumstances all work together to bring me to the place of fellowship with You, to the place where I study Your Word to know You better.' Prophesy that extraordinary fire shall be rekindled in your life again.

- Pray and banish every lukewarm attitude from your life and from your family.

- Decree and declare that every satanic altar raised against your spiritual altar be destroyed.

- Prophesy and decree that your spiritual life will not crumble. Decree that whenever you travail in prayer like a pregnant woman, you shall bring forth and that there shall be no abortion or miscarriage.

## MY PROPHETIC DECLARATION

Heavenly Father of mercy! You are the Strong Tower that I run to and I am saved. You are my Shelter and my Shade from the heat of the day.. You are my Rock, my Refuge and Hiding-place from the storms of life. I declare that my heart will serve You fervently and my spirit will follow after You consistently for You are my Redeemer and in You I safely trust. I will not grow weary. I will not become faint I will not become tired in the place of prayer and in the time of studying Your Word. In Your Presence there is liberty, there is security and peace. Therefore, I decree that as I am travailing in prayers, You will assist me to bring forth in Jesus Name! I decree there shall be no abortion or miscarriage.

Your fire O Lord burns inside of me. The zeal of Your House and of Your Kingdom consumes me. My relationship with You will not become lukewarm. I declare that the pressures of this world will not choke Your Word out of my life and that of my household. I declare that nothing that happens around me will cause me to surrender my time of prayer or fellowship with You in Jesus' Name! Because I serve You and worship You, my heavens will not be shut up. Since I am called by Your Name, I renounce all carelessness and lukewarmness in my life henceforth in Jesus' Name! I decree that my spiritual life is hereby fortified by the power of the Holy Ghost. No more complacency and no lukewarmness in Jesus Name!

# 18

## LORD, DEFEND YOUR WORD IN MY LIFE

*Not one of all the Lord's good promises to the house of Israel failed; every one was fulfilled.*

Joshua 21:45 (NIV)

*...for I am alert and active, watching over My Word to perform it.*

Jeremiah 1:12b (AMP)

*.... There shall none of My words be deferred any more, but the word which I have spoken shall be performed, says the Lord God.*

Ezekiel 12:28b (AMP)

*So shall My word be that goes forth out of My mouth: it shall not return to Me void [without producing any effect, useless], but it shall accomplish that which I please and purpose, and it shall prosper in the thing for which I sent it.*

Isaiah 55:11 (AMP)

## REFLECTION

A Bible commentary wisely purports that the Word of God is not just a collection of words from God or just a vehicle for communicating ideas. Rather it is, living, life-changing and dynamic as it works in us. Therefore, not only should you listen to or decree His Word, but also allow His Word to shape and direct the course of your life. When God speaks a Word, it is guaranteed to come to pass. Joshua, the man who took on the responsibility to bring the nation of Israel into the Promised Land following the death of Moses, records that not a single one of the promises that God gave Israel was left unfulfilled! Not one! Every Word that God spoke into the life of Abraham, Isaac and Jacob was fulfilled to the letter!

Isaiah the prophet captured this in the 55th chapter of Isaiah stating clearly that every Word that God speaks will prosper and perform the thing concerning which He (God) sent it. I encourage you to make a note of God's promises to you and regularly remind yourself of these promises. When things around you seem to go from bad to worse or things fail to happen as you expect them to, remind yourself of His promises, remind yourself of His Word to you concerning your circumstances. Rest therefore in the confidence that not a single one of those promises, not a single one of those Words will go unfulfilled!

When people around you, including your loved ones, peers or work colleagues, look at you and make a mockery of your faith in God, remind yourself of God's Word to you. When you appear before a panel, or a judge over a matter for which you have been unjustly accused, bring to remembrance God's Word for your life.

When you are faced with that impossible situation and people stand and watch afar off, waiting to hear that you have been destroyed or that you have been buried by that situation; go back and read the Word, remind yourself of His promises concerning you. Remind yourself that not a single one of His Word concerning you will go unfulfilled! Let this be a guarantee for you that you will be saved from that challenging situation! Philippians 1:28 (AMP) tells us "And do not [for a moment] be frightened or intimidated in anything by your opponents and adversaries, for such [constancy and fearlessness] will be a clear sign (proof and seal) to them of [their impending] destruction, but [a sure token and evidence] of your deliverance and salvation, and that from God." Call on God to defend His Word throughout your lifetime! Remember it shall come to pass.

## PRAYER POINTS

- Call on the name of the Lord, remind Him that none who put their trust in Him will ever be put to shame, say Lord, defend your WORD in my life!

- Pray that none of the promises of God in your life will be deferred or delayed.

- Tell your heavenly Father that you are stepping out of this situation and allowing Him to take control and defend His Word and His Name.

- Ask the Lord to defend His Name in your place of work – in particular your job and your position. Ask Him to defend His Word in your family.

- Ask the Lord to defend His Word in the life of your children, in their schooling and in the company they keep. Ask the Lord to defend His Word over them as they commute to and from school. Ask the Lord to defend His Name in their lives when enjoying social activities – particularly when away from home or in the company of others

- Thank the Lord that every Word He has spoken

concerning you will prosper in the thing for which He sent it.

- Thank the Lord that His Word is alive and active; thank Him for keeping watch over His Word to ensure that every Word that He has spoken concerning you is performed.

## MY PROPHETIC DECLARATION

Lord God of heaven, I believe Your Word is alert and active! Your Word is sharper than the sharpest knife, cutting deep into our innermost thoughts and desires; it exposes us for what we really are. Therefore, I decree that the effect of every preached Word I have received in all areas of my life shall be greatly multiplied. I declare that every Word of life spoken concerning my household shall be fulfilled. God's Word spoken concerning me will prosper in everything for which the Word is sent. None of God's promises concerning me will suffer delay or be deferred any longer. My Lord and my God shall publicly defend and justify His Word and His Name in my life. For God Himself is watching over His Word concerning me and will perform it in the mighty name of Jesus.

Because of the written Word of my heavenly Father, all the handwriting of ordinances that were previously against me and my household are now null and void. My Saviour and Redeemer has taken every evil pronouncement against me to the Cross and has nailed them there. Therefore, I will not be put to shame because I have put my trust in His unfailing Word of life. I declare that the Lord will defend His Word concerning my job. He will defend His Word concerning my children; concerning my future; concerning my church; concerning my business; concerning every aspect of my life (name other areas) in Jesus Name! I decree that anywhere people call on the name of the Lord, there shall be a free and full expression of the ministry of His Word and the Spirit in Jesus Name!

# 19

## CONQUERING MARITAL ATTACKS

*For this reason a man will leave his father and mother and be united to his wife, and they will become one flesh.*

Genesis 2:24 (NIV)

*They will build houses and dwell in them; they will plant vineyards and eat their fruit...*

Isaiah 65:21 (NIV)

*For the Lord, the God of Israel says: I hate divorce and marital separation and him who covers his garment [his wife] with violence. Therefore keep a watch upon your spirit [that it may be controlled by My Spirit], that you deal not treacherously and faithlessly with your marriage mate.*

Malachi 2:16 (AMP)

*You cry out, "Why doesn't the Lord accept my worship?" I'll tell you why! Because the Lord witnessed the vows you and your wife made when you were young. But you have been unfaithful to her, though she remained your faithful partner, the wife of your marriage vows*

Malachi 2:14 (NLT)

## REFLECTION

Every marriage is constantly targeted by the enemy for one simple reason… the family unit is God's foundation for society. This is the same reason Adam's union with Eve was attacked by the devil in the Garden of Eden. If the foundation is solid, then all of society will be sound. The Bible says if the root is holy, then the rest of the tree will also be holy "For if the roots of the tree are holy, the branches will be, too" (Romans 11:16c NLT). The success of any family unit is a confirmation of the devils failure and defeat in the battle between light and darkness.

I ask every person reading this book, to take comfort in the fact that the difficulties you may be experiencing in your marriage are not uncommon and should not be a surprise to you. You may think that your spouse is the cause of all the problems but that is exactly what the enemy wants you to think. The adversary wants you to pick a fight and a quarrel with your spouse, the very one whom you love when in actual fact; he is the one you need to fight and destroy! Please take note - those fights are cleverly designed to separate you from your wife or husband, and therefore crack the foundation that forms the bedrock of your family unit. Do not be unwise, do not be ignorant of the devices of the enemy, allow him no foothold in your marriage.

I urge you take a stand against every threat and attack on your marriage or the home that you have laboured to build. God has promised that you will live in houses that you have built and you will eat of the vine that you have planted. Have you laboured with your spouse or betrothed one for a long time; are you now faced with the possibility of not enjoying the imminent harvest?

Perhaps you are in a place where it is a struggle for you to openly worship God? Or do you feel like the heavens are closed towards you? Check your relationship with your spouse, is there any act of treachery that the enemy has subtly sown into your relationship? You were designed to be with your spouse for ever as one, anything that seeks to separate you can only cause a tear. Here is some news for you - since a tear is never straight, there will always be parts missing from both halves of the paper; even while still attached to each other. This implies that the process of the tear may leave behind wounds that will probably never heal. God doesn't want this to happen, therefore you must rise up and take a stand for your home and extinguish every sign of a threat or attack to your relationship; for God is love. Don't be satisfied with just 'sellotaping' or 'gluing' over the tear – it will only become a weak spot and be prone to constant damage. Rather grab the hand of your beloved partner right now and step into the place of prayer – pray for your marriage – do it now!

## PRAYER POINTS

- Pray and ask God for a super covering over your marriage, your relationship with your spouse and your relationship with your children. Renounce any demonic covenant working against your marital life.

- Pray and cover your home and your marriage with the Blood of Jesus. Pray that the Blood of the new covenant will be a standard against the enemy in your marriage.

- Pray concerning that situation you have identified as a threat or an attack to your marriage i.e. financial issues, inconsiderate behaviours, self-centredness, mutual disrespect (name the situation and the issues); pray that the situation will be dissolved by His mercies.

- Pray and ask God for wisdom to help you discern the working of the enemy in your home, that you will quickly recognise every threat to your home for what it is and not fight against your spouse.

- Pray and tear down everything that manifests as an attack against you, your spouse and against your home. Declare that you will both stand firm against every attack of the devil!

- Pray that the Lord will deliver you from every situation that will subtly cause you to be unfaithful to your marriage vows.

- Pray and take authority over all communication problems in your home. Decree that you will adopt a communication style that will build up your home and edify your partner and not tear each other down in Jesus' Name!

## MY PROPHETIC DECLARATION

I declare that my marriage is safe and sound! I dissolve and scatter everything that is a threat to my home in Jesus' Name. I decree and declare that every attack on my marriage has failed; for every evil plan and wicked accusation against my marriage will not succeed. Surely there is no enchantment against my marriage, neither is there any divination against me. My husband/wife is the bone of my bones and flesh of my flesh. Therefore, I declare that my home is stable, firmly built on the solid Rock and is under the mighty arm of the Lord.

Since our marriage/relationship is built on nothing less than the Blood of Jesus, no weapon formed or fashioned against my marriage shall prosper; no arrow of the enemy against my home will reach its mark in the Name of Jesus! I make a pronouncement that every situation that will cause arguments and disunity between my spouse and I, be dissolved by the power of the Holy Spirit.

I affirm that the Lord will help me to recognise every form of subtle attack against my marriage. I decree as Jesus is the firm foundation on which my marriage is built, that no arguments, misunderstandings or misrepresentations will have a foothold in my home in Jesus Name!

## SUCCEEDING DESPITE
## DISCOURAGEMENT

*Therefore do not cast away your confidence, which has great reward. For you have need of endurance, so that after you have done the will of God, you may receive the promise:*

Hebrews 10:35-36 (NKJV)

*You will bring justice to the orphans and the oppressed, so mere people can no longer terrify them*

Psalm 10:18 (NLT)

*No-one will be able to stand up against you all the days of your life. As I was with Moses, so I will be with you; I will never leave you nor forsake you. Be strong and courageous, because you will lead these people to inherit the land I swore to their forefathers to give them.*

Joshua 1:5-6 (NIV)

*Jesus looked at them and said, "With man this is impossible, but with God all things are possible.*

Matthew 19:26 (NIV)

**REFLECTION**

Have you ever started out on a road never walked by others or embarked on a journey via a route less fancied by most people? It is very easy to get discouraged, especially if you listen to the opinions of "small minds." These are the people who will try to keep you "boxed up" in the status quo; they will attempt to keep you caged in mediocrity – the place where they think you belong.

When you are a pace setter, out to do something different from the ordinary, people may impress upon you their stereotypical thinking of how you might not succeed with your venture. However, God has promised to vindicate you with success on all sides. He will bring you the truth so that you will no longer be held bound or oppressed by "mere men."

God has given His word to free us from the opinions of men that have held us bound. His Word tells us that all things are possible. Yes, listen to the rendition of Mark 9:23 in the New Living Translation…"What do you mean, 'If I can'?" Jesus asked. "Anything is possible if a person believes." Have you received inspiration to do something different or something new? Do not say I can't! Do not be held back because somebody said you can't. Have you been giving audience to the voices of discouragement that constantly tell you that you can't do it? Well, God says you can. Perhaps someone has told you that it can only be done in a certain way, and now you are beginning to agree with these voices of discouragement. Remember you are not a copy of anyone but created in the image of God and He says you have dominion over the earth. So "yes you can", Jesus said in Mark 9:23 "what do you mean if I can" everything is possible if you can only believe God's Word.

I bet you're thinking "it has never been done before", I say so what? Yes, it has never been done that way, so what? Yes, it has never been done by someone from your family line or from your race, so what? Yes, it has never happened that quickly, so what? Tell that to Barack Obama! You have surely reached the point of stagnation when all you do is listen to those voices of discouragement.

I am sure the current president of the "greatest country" in the world had many opportunities to back down and quit his dream, I am sure there were people telling him constantly that it was impossible for a black man to be president of the United States of America. I am sure even members of his family tried to talk him out of the presidential race and he probably had plenty of opportunity in his quiet moments to question whether or not he could do it.

I have personally seen pictures of a host of pastors praying and laying hands on President Barack Obama. I am convinced that he drew encouragement from these men of God around him and from the Word of God. He believed that "change" was possible and that a new era was imminent. The rest as they say is now history!

My challenge to you as you read this book is what do you mean "if you can"? All things are possible to him/her that believeth. All you need is a faith-lift. Believe God's Word of promise and aim higher for a greater outcome. Invite Him into your life and into that situation and take a step of faith to activate that change, because with God all things are possible and you can overcome every voice of discouragement. That means everything!

## PRAYER POINTS

- Pray and ask God to adequately equip you to triumph over all situations such as persecution and discouragement that can hinder you from fulfilling your purpose on earth.

- Ask the Lord to break down every barrier of opposition against you. Pray that the Lord will take away the oppression of mere men around you.

- Lift up your voice in prayer and say "Lord, make me a pacesetter in my generation and make me a vessel of change in my generation and for my posterity."

- Ask the Lord who makes the impossible possible, the One who makes a way in the wilderness to give you the strength and courage to do the new thing that you have been inspired to do.

- Ask the Lord to distance you from the oppression of mere men, that you will no longer be terrorised by their criticism and their discouraging opinions.

- Take authority over every lie of Satan. Pray and ask God to send you people who will help you fulfil the burning desire of a new thing in your heart.

- Prophesy that you can do all things through Christ who strengthens you; whether in your job or in your family or whether it is the actualisation of a major new thing in life.

## MY PROPHETIC DECLARATION

I declare that I will no longer be held in bondage by the opinion of men. Even though I walk through the valley of the shadow of death, I fear no evil.

I believe discouragement is just a shadow and I will not be discouraged. The oppressive words of the enemies against my progress are taken away in Jesus' Name! I decree according to God's Word because I believe that nothing shall be impossible to me. I take authority over every lie of the devil. For the Lord has kept me from condemnation knowing that I shall find grace and mercy over every discouraging situation in my time of need. I decree I shall walk confidently in the land of the living to wholeheartedly worship my God.

I will do new things. I will walk new roads. I will not be held down by status quo and by accepted traditions and norms. I will be free from the opinion of men. I am free from every spirit of discouragement to fulfil my destiny and achieve even the impossible in Jesus Name!

I declare that I am strong and courageous, for my heavenly Father shall confound every expectation of demonic forces against my life! They shall be like wind and be blown away. I will leap over every demonic wall! I will be a pacesetter for my generation for I dare to be different.

# 21

## DESTROYING MISCARRIAGES & BARRENNESS

*Worship the Lord your God and His blessing will be on your food and water. I will take away sickness from among you, and none will miscarry or be barren in your land. I will give you a full life span*

Exodus 23:25-26 (NIV)

*He shall be like a tree Planted by the rivers of water, that brings forth its fruit in its season, whose leaf also shall not wither; and whatever he does shall prosper*

Psalm 1: 3 (NKJV)

*You shall be blessed above all peoples; there shall not be male or female barren among you, or among your cattle*

Deuteronomy 7:14 (AMP)

**He settles the barren woman in her home as a happy mother of children. Praise the LORD**

Psalm 113:9 (NIV)

**REFLECTION**

Recently, fertility problems in women - namely miscarriages and barrenness, seem to have become very prevalent. One of the reasons for this could be the handiwork of principalities and powers of darkness. You must therefore, bind them in the Name of Jesus, knowing fully well that whatsoever you bind on earth, will be bound in heaven.

Perhaps as you read this book, you have a "should have", "could have" or "would have" tale to share with anyone who cares to listen. Maybe your "should have" tale is how you can overcome miscarriages and barrenness and become fruitful. Regardless of what should have been but has not been, be reminded that God is the God who gives life in abundance. Your circumstances may be like the woman in the Bible with the issue of blood for twelve years. You may have been battling with miscarriages or infertility since you got married. Maybe friends and relatives around you have despised you and even tagged you with derogatory names. Perhaps you are in a relationship where you have been given a 'deadline' to give birth to a child or else a replacement would be sought. Has this made you depressed, discouraged and frustrated? Has confusion also set in because doctors have diagnosed in their reports that your conception is impossible or that your constant miscarriages stem from an unknown cause.

Like Hannah in the Bible, have you been repeatedly provoked and mocked? Don't lose hope, wipe your tears I have good news for you and it is breaking news! With God nothing is impossible! That miscarriage shall cease and you will no longer be tagged as barren. I know of a lady who suffered miscarriages, after years of marriage; however, she set her face like a flint and stood firm on God's Word with fervent prayers. Today, she's is a mother of three wonderful children! I also know of another lady whom friends tagged as an "empty box of matches", today God has changed her story as He changed the story of the woman with the issue of blood. When this woman heard that Jesus was in town, with a profound faith she quickly made an effort to get to the Greatest Physician when all the physicians of this world failed her. In a day and within split seconds, she was healed of twelve years of non-stop bleeding (Mark 5:25-34)! As a woman, you will surely know what that means.

Yes, God may have promised you children in His Word and perhaps even by prophetic revelation. Please believe me when I say you will still need to pray and believe God earnestly in order to receive the promised blessing. Isaac received the promise made to his father, Abraham to become the father of many nations but he waited 20 years after marrying his wife Rebecca before he had any children. He was aware of the promises of God and perhaps he waited the first 19 years confident that God's promise will definitely come through however, a time came when he realised he had to take action. "Isaac prayed to the Lord on behalf of his wife, because she was barren. The Lord answered his prayer, and his wife Rebecca became pregnant" (Genesis 25:21 NIV). Another version says that he "entreated the Lord" concerning his wife's barrenness and the Lord answered him. Perhaps you have held on to the promise of God for your life and nothing has happened. Or you may have actually become pregnant a few times and have lost the baby before full term. I tell you of a truth, the time has come for some radical steps to be taken to "entreat" the Lord either for yourself or for your wife! Go to God with His Word. Remind Him that He has promised to settle you or your wife in your home as happy parents of children, that He has promised that none shall be barren in your land. Remind Him that Zion did not bring forth prematurely but only after due time of labour. You need to remind Him that it was as soon as Zion went into labour that she brought forth her children, then pray and entreat Him to bring His Word to pass in your life and in the lives of your loved ones!

One of the blessings (or if you like to call them benefits) of serving God is fruitfulness. If you read through the entire Bible, you will not find a single woman who was barren apart from David's wife who despised David for dancing and praising the Lord. You can actually see that her barrenness was a direct consequence of her refusal to worship God and her spite for those who worshipped God. Even Jezebel, the "queen of wickedness" had the privilege of having children. This tells me that if you serve God, and worship God, it is impossible for you to remain barren or unfruitful.

## PRAYER POINTS

- Pray and command every satanic curse of miscarriages and barrenness in your life and your family to be uprooted and overthrown permanently.

- Pray and command every evil chain to be broken, every chord or padlock, tying your womb/fallopian tubes to be destroyed in Jesus' Name! Ask God to rebuild all desolations in your family background and that of your partner.

- Pray that no part of your reproductive system shall wither. Decree that your womb/your wife's womb will open up, come alive and be viable to receive seed and conceive a child.

- Pray that your body will be like a fruitful vine,

planted beside rivers of water, bringing forth fruit in season. Prophesy that you shall be as a fruitful vine.

- Decree that you will not miscarry and that there shall be no threatening abortions. Prophesy that your pregnancy will come to full term and you will not go into premature labour in Jesus' Name.

- Pray that when your pregnancy has come to full term, your labour will be short and effective for as soon as Zion went into labour, she brought forth her child. Prophesy that the midwives shall habour no evil for you.

- Pray and decree that on God's due date for your pregnancy, there shall be no complications. The living shall proceed out of the living and there shall be shouts and tears of joy to the glory of God!

## MY PROPHETIC DECLARATION

I stand upon the Rock of Ages and I attack every kingdom of darkness, all demonic covenants and powers and principalities that have held my womb from conceiving in Jesus Name! I command all demonic hands holding on to my womb, my fallopian tubes and my reproductive organs to loose their hold over my life and that of my loved ones. Heavenly Father, let them be ashamed and confounded that seek after my fruitfulness. Through the Blood of the everlasting covenant, the blood that speaks better things than the blood of Abel, Lord Jesus, let this blood speak restoration and peace to every cause of miscarriages and barrenness in my life. I hold on to this blood and I declare that my body is alive, my womb is alive and my reproductive system is functioning in Jesus' Name. I prophesy that I will not cast my young before time and I will not miscarry! Threatening abortion is not my portion and I shall not be barren. Instead, I shall carry my baby in my womb to full term.

I declare that I am like a fruitful vine planted besides the rivers of water, I bring forth my fruit in due season. I prophesy that on God's due date for my delivery, I shall bring forth my baby in peace in Jesus' Name! For no weapon formed against my delivery date shall prosper and no enchantment or divination will work in the labour room. I declare that the living shall proceed out of the living and mother and baby shall be well and give glory to You O Lord.

By God's amazing grace, my children and my loved ones will possess the gates of our enemies in Jesus Name!

# OTHER BOOKS BY
# BENEDICTA OLAGUNJU

To purchase this book and
other books by the author,
please contact:
pstmrsbolagunju@aol.com
or telephone +447704 590789 / +447951 408581

# ABOUT THE AUTHOR

Benedicta Olagunju is an established international conference speaker, a prophetic preacher and expositor of the Word of God.

She is the president of the Women With a Purpose Ministry of Focus International Christian Centre. Benedicta holds a Diploma in Social Work and a Bachelor of Arts (Hons) in Applied Social Studies. She is an adept writer and counsellor in the areas of prayer, relationships, marriage and daily living.

Benedicta is married to Pastor B.B., a dynamic preacher and senior pastor of FICC. Their marriage is blessed with wonderful children.